# PAKISTAN

BY WILLIAM GOODWIN

LUCENT
BOOKS®

THOMSON
™
GALE

San Diego • Detroit • New York • San Francisco • Cleveland
New Haven, Conn. • Waterville, Maine • London • Munich

## TITLES IN THE MODERN NATIONS OF THE WORLD SERIES INCLUDE:

| | | |
|---|---|---|
| Afghanistan | Greece | Russia |
| Australia | Haiti | Saudi Arabia |
| Austria | India | Scotland |
| Brazil | Iran | Somalia |
| Canada | Italy | South Africa |
| China | Japan | South Korea |
| Cuba | Jordan | Sweden |
| England | Kenya | Switzerland |
| Ethiopia | Mexico | Taiwan |
| France | Norway | United States |
| Germany | Pakistan | |

*This book is dedicated to the members of the band Junoon, delivering Pakistan's message of hope, peace, and sanity to the world.*

On cover: Street scene in Islamabad

*For more information, contact*
Lucent Books
27500 Drake Rd.
Farmington Hills, MI 48331-3535
Or you can visit our Internet site at http://www.gale.com

**LIBRARY OF CONGRESS CATALOGING-IN-PUBLICATION DATA**

Goodwin, William.
    Pakistan / by William Goodwin.
      p.   cm. — (Modern nations of the world)
Summary: Discusses the geography, climate, population, plants and animals, history, religion, culture, and future of Pakistan.
Includes bibliographical references and index.

    ISBN 1-59018-218-9 (hardback: alk. paper)

  1. Pakistan—Juvenile literature.  [1. Pakistan.]  I. Title.  II. Series.
    DS376.9 .G66 2002
    954.91—dc21

                             2002 001 911

# CONTENTS

# INTRODUCTION

## "LAND OF THE PURE"

The word *Pakistan* means "Land of the Pure," but for the half century of its existence this young country has found it difficult to live up to its name. In the broad valley of the Indus River, home of one of humanity's earliest civilizations and the heartland of modern Pakistan, hardship haunts the inhabitants. Since the birth of Pakistan in 1947, the country has been hampered by wars with its neighbors, persistent domestic violence, poverty, floods, droughts, a devastated economy, overpopulation, and corruption. But this ancient land is also blessed by a dynamic and religious people, abundant water, excellent access to the sea, and inspiring geography that includes many of the world's tallest mountains.

Pakistan and India both gained their independence from Britain in 1947, and before the end of their first year as independent countries they had already fought their first war with each other. Pakistan has gone to war with India several times since then, and the failure to settle its disputes with India has diverted much of Pakistan's meager resources to the military. The resulting shortage of funds for education, health, and infrastructure has created a daunting set of challenges for the rapidly increasing population.

Pakistan has one of the highest illiteracy rates in Asia, with 64 percent of adults (77 percent of women) unable to read and write. About half of the people do not have access to health services or safe drinking water. And these are not the only discouraging statistics contributing to the country's mounting social problems. A quadrupling of the population during Pakistan's first fifty years of existence and a lack of economic opportunities in the rural areas have prompted heavy migration to the cities, where sprawling suburbs with minimal services create conditions conducive to crime and social unrest.

But Pakistan's sprawling cities are also home to a growing and influential middle class. Educated, aware, and longing for prosperity and stability, these Pakistanis take a dim view of the country's violent extremists. Pakistan's middle class is far more interested in working on the difficult transition to the modern world of high technology and international markets than in waging war or sponsoring international terrorism.

Besides a growing middle class, Pakistan's hot, crowded cities are also home to millions of uneducated and desperately poor people. An undertone of violence vibrates through these masses, and it is amplified by the many monuments dedicated to Pakistan's first atomic bomb. The more extreme elements in this almost entirely Muslim population feel a kinship with Muslim militants in other parts of the world—a kinship that sometimes translates into support for Islamic terrorist organizations. Adding more fuel to the fires of social unrest, many Pakistanis are itching for another war with India over the disputed territory of Kashmir, the longest continuous military engagement found anywhere in modern history. Thus, despite the promise and potential of the young nation of Pakistan, this undercurrent of violence makes it one of the most volatile countries of the twenty-first century.

*Pakistan's dynamic and beautiful geography includes Trich Mir, located in the country's westernmost mountain range.*

# 1

# FROM THE SEA TO THE MOUNTAINS

Because of its location and geography, for millions of years Pakistan has been the gateway between the riches of southern Asia and the relatively desolate territories of central Asia and the Middle East. The people and even the plants and animals of modern Pakistan are a reflection of the country's location as a crossroads between India and the rest of the world. The same geographical features that have done so much to shape life and culture in Pakistan have created a country of uninhabitable deserts, fertile farmlands, broad rivers, and lush valleys enclosed by some of the world's tallest mountains.

## LOCATION

Pakistan is situated in the western part of the Indian subcontinent, bordering Afghanistan and Iran to the west, India to the east, Afghanistan and China to the north, and the Arabian Sea to the south. The country occupies 307,374 square miles, making it a little larger than the state of Texas, a quarter the size of its eastern neighbor India. It has about 500 miles of coastline on the Arabian Sea.

## THE GREAT MOUNTAINS OF PAKISTAN

Where northern Pakistan meets Asia, the land has buckled, folded, and tilted up to form a series of mountain ranges that include some of the tallest mountains in the world. The mountains, many of them clad in immense glaciers, enclose lush valleys like Kashmir and Swat, and drier, higher, sparsely populated valleys like Gilgit and Hunza.

Pakistan's great mountains separate the country from China to the north and Afghanistan to the north and west.

The mountains consist of three distinct ranges: the Himalayas, the Karakoram, and the Hindu Kush. The westernmost end of the Himalayan chain pushes into northeastern Pakistan from India. Northwest of the Himalayas rise the peaks of the Karakoram Range, and the Hindu Kush mountains rise northwest of the Karakoram and extend westward into Afghanistan.

Pakistan has seven of the sixteen tallest peaks in Asia, and forty of the world's fifty highest mountains. The tallest peak is K2, which at 28,251 feet is the second-highest mountain in the world. In the district of Baltistan in the extreme north of the country, forty-six peaks exceed 20,000 feet. The region's technically difficult and inhospitable peaks attract mountaineers from all over the world, which has resulted in more climbing deaths in Pakistan than in any other country.

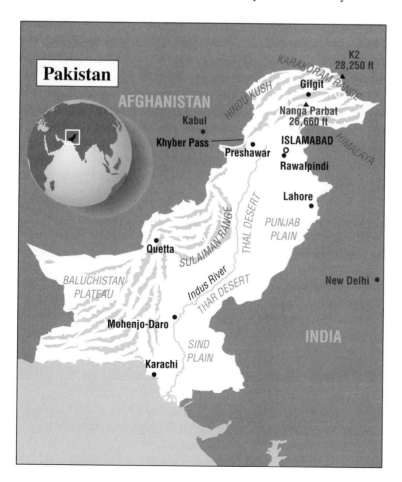

## CLIMBING K2: THE MOUNTAIN OF MOUNTAINS

In northern Pakistan, rows of jagged mountains reach to the sky, and the most spectacular of these mountain groups is the Karakoram Range. There, far from human habitation and unknown to the outside world until 1856, a giant mountain known as K2 straddles the border between Pakistan and China. Named *K2* because it was the second major peak of the Karakorams to be identified, this 28,251-foot mountain is second in height only to Mount Everest.

K2's awesome mass looms over a frigid, treeless valley known as Concordia. Four of the earth's tallest mountains sit within a thirteen-mile radius, making this the largest concentration of the world's highest peaks. Though almost two hundred people have successfully reached the top of K2, dozens of others have died on K2's steep slopes since a British surveyor discovered it.

K2, also called Godwin Austen and (locally) Dapsang, was discovered and measured in 1856 by Colonel T.G. Montgomerie of the Survey of India, the arm of the British government that mapped the subcontinent. The name *Godwin Austen* is derived from Colonel H.H. Godwin-Austen, a nineteenth-century English geographer who was the first to fully survey the approach to Concordia during the 1860s and may have been the first European to reach the base of K2 (Montgomerie had made his measurements from the top of a distant pass).

Mountaineers who have been there agree that the peaks of the Karakoram Range are among the most difficult and dangerous of all the world's high mountains. The first attempts to climb K2 took place during the final years of the nineteenth century, but one after another they all failed. Then, in 1954, an Italian expedition came to Pakistan to try its luck on K2. Despite the death of one member of the expedition during the ascent, the group persisted, and on July 31, 1954, two Italian men, Lino Lacedelli and Achille Compagnoni, became the first to reach the summit of K2.

Pakistan's mountains have more glaciers than any other mountain area on Earth. For example, the Karakoram glaciers cover as much as 37 percent of the land area, far more than the Himalayas (17 percent) or Alps (22 percent). The most outstanding of these rivers of ice is the 38-mile-long Baltoro glacier, which covers an area of 496 square miles.

Most of the mountain passes in northern Pakistan are higher than the highest peaks of the Alps, and as a result, the Karakoram Highway linking Pakistan to China is the highest trade route in the world. The Karakoram Highway was a strategic project designed to emphasize friendly relations between both countries and to counter the alliance between India and the Soviet Union. The highway passes through very dangerous and difficult terrain, following steep valleys and river gorges. Rockfalls and landslides frequently destroy parts of the road so that travel is often blocked for days.

In the extreme northwest, the Gilgit, Hunza, and other valleys formed by the tall mountains tend to be harsh places to live and are thus sparsely populated. The western and southern valleys of Chitral, Dir, Kaghan, and Swat, however, have numerous rivers and lakes, forests of pine and junipers, a great variety of fauna and flora, and comparatively greater numbers of people. South of the high mountains, the ranges gradually become hills until finally the earth flattens into the plains of the North-West Frontier province and the Punjab, Pakistan's two northernmost provinces.

*Because of its forbidding height the rugged Karakoram Highway offers travelers a dangerous journey, including occasional glacial flooding.*

A range of smaller but nevertheless rugged, dry mountains runs from the western Hindu Kush down to the Baluchistan province along the border of Pakistan and Afghanistan. These mountains achieved notoriety during the American-led attacks on Afghanistan when the Taliban and al-Qaeda forces used these areas to hide and escape into Pakistan. The Khyber Pass forms the most important overland route through these mountains.

### THE GREAT RIVERS

Pakistan's mountains are drained by several large river systems. The valleys and plains through which these rivers flow are among the most fertile lands on Earth. But all is not green in Pakistan. In addition to the mountain ranges, plains, plateaus, and valleys where the monsoons bring plentiful rain, the country also has vast areas that are arid and sparsely populated.

The largest and by far the most important of Pakistan's rivers is the mighty Indus, the sixth-largest river system in the world. It divides the country in half as it runs fifteen hundred miles from the Himalayas near the Chinese border southward through the densely populated Indus plain. The Indus ends in the Arabian Sea, where it forms the fifth-largest river delta in the world.

### PLATEAUS, DESERTS, PLAINS, AND BEACHES

A fertile plateau crosses the country from west to east southward from the tall northern mountains. This plateau extends from the Peshawar valley in the west across the northern Punjab, where Pakistan's capital, Islamabad, stands near the border with India.

South of this fertile plateau, the terrain gradually turns to desert. To the west is the desolate Baluchistan plateau, which reaches into southern Iran. To the east below the Punjab, the great expanse of the Thar Desert spreads almost to the Arabian Sea. Between these two desert areas is the fertile Indus plain, Pakistan's heartland where most of the people live and where most of the country's food is grown. Though this region gets little rain, it is well irrigated by a vast system of canals.

The southern coast, washed by the warm waters of the Arabian Sea, has busy harbors, sandy beaches, lagoons, and mangrove swamps. Other than the sprawling industrial city of Karachi, the country's only deepwater port, most of Pakistan's coast is undeveloped.

## CLIMATE

Pakistan experiences some of the most extreme temperatures on Earth, from 120 degrees Fahrenheit in the Sindh region during summer, to -55 degrees in the northern mountain ranges during winter. Drought is a major problem in some areas, but in others annual floods are the major problem. During the summer months devastating hurricanes (called typhoons in southern Asia) sometimes strike the heavily populated coastal regions around Karachi.

Pakistan's massive northern mountains are one of the major influences on the country's weather patterns. For months each year, huge moisture-filled weather systems called monsoons blow up from the Indian Ocean. Blocked by the wall of mountains, the monsoons deposit most of their heavy rains on the plateau below the mountains.

Exposed to the monsoons, the southern slopes of the Hindu Kush mountains and the valleys and hills south of them receive thirty to fifty inches of rain each year. But although some of Pakistan receives monsoon rains, much of the country is arid. Even the Karakoram and Himalayan mountain ranges are relatively dry since they are blocked to the south from the monsoons by the Hindu Kush mountains; consequently, they receive less precipitation than most deserts.

Almost as dry as the far northern mountains, the province of Baluchistan in western Pakistan receives an average annual rainfall of only eight inches. And the Thar Desert sometimes goes for years without any rain at all.

Pakistanis are fond of describing their weather as having three seasons: the cold season, the hot season, and the wet season. The entire country experiences cold weather from the middle of December to March. During that season the humidity is low and, except on the coast, the nights often reach freezing. From April to June the land gradually heats up until conditions are almost unbearable. By June, daytime temperatures in the interior of the country often exceed one hundred degrees Fahrenheit. The wet season begins in July when the southwest monsoons arrive and the dry air becomes saturated with humidity as heavy rains fall almost every day for at least two months. The monsoons begin tapering off toward the end of August, and by the middle of September the rain has stopped. Daytime highs in October drop into the nineties, and the nights become pleasant. Pakistanis enjoy their most comfortable weather during the postmonsoon months of October and November.

### FLORA AND FAUNA

The naturally occurring plant life in Pakistan's lowlands is patchy, consisting mostly of scattered clumps of grass and stunted woodlands. As the terrain rises, however, large coniferous forests exist in the places too remote or steep for logging, and in many places the lower slopes are carpeted with grass and wildflowers much of the year. Along the Arabian Sea coastline in the south, many immense mangrove swamps, prime breeding grounds for many kinds of sea life, are found along the huge river estuaries and deltas.

Because of Pakistan's widely varied topography and climate, the country is endowed with a large number of mammals, reptiles, amphibians, birds, and fish. According to the World Wildlife Federation (WWF), Pakistan's fauna includes 188 species of mammals, including bears, otters, deer, mountain sheep, jackals, and endangered snow leopards. Bird life is numerous and varied (668 species, including

*Crocodiles in their marshy habitat may become a rarity in Pakistan because of habitat degradation.*

#  INDUS RIVER DOLPHINS

River dolphins, found only in the Indus, several other large rivers in Asia, and the Amazon, never go into the sea. Indus River dolphins are gray-brown, with stocky bodies and large, paddle-shaped flippers. They have long beaks, large teeth, and the familiar "smiling" mouth line of most dolphins. River dolphins range in size from 6 to 8 feet long and 180 to 200 pounds. They eat crustaceans and small fish and live to about thirty years of age. Unlike most ocean-dwelling dolphins, however, they lack a large dorsal fin. Also unlike ocean dolphins, these river dolphins travel either as couples or as individuals. They often swim on their sides in shallow water, one fin touching the bottom, while their tail moves from side to side. On their sides, they trail one flipper through the muddy riverbed, which helps them find food.

Like dolphins everywhere, they use echolocation (biological sonar) to "visualize" their surroundings. In the case of Indus River dolphins, echolocation literally takes the place of sight because their eyes are underdeveloped and have no lenses. They can sense only light and dark, which is sufficient since the rivers are so murky.

Following the construction of numerous dams beginning in the 1930s, this formerly common mammal has become greatly endangered. Besides the dams, which split the dolphin population into small groups, changed the river habitat from fast to slow moving, and impeded natural patterns of migration, accidental capture in fishing nets and intentional hunting for meat, oil, and traditional medicine have also reduced the numbers of remaining river dolphins. Where once they could be found in the Indus and its tributaries from the sea to the foothills of the Himalayas, today there are fewer than one thousand Indus River dolphins remaining. Widespread legal protections were enacted during the 1970s, and a river dolphin population in a preserve in the Sindh province appears to be the best hope for the survival of these rare mammals.

*Wildlife workers soothe an Indus River dolphin.*

migratory birds). Freshwater dolphins live in the Indus River, and the sprawling delta supports a population of marsh crocodiles. Pakistan's coastline teems with many species of fish, sharks, shellfish, and sea turtles, and its rivers and lakes are home to hundreds of fish species.

Pakistan has become increasingly concerned with the continuous and progressive loss, fragmentation, and degradation of its natural habitats, a set of problems that have accelerated during the 1980s and 1990s due to the country's rapidly growing population. In many places only patches of forests remain, and along with most of the rangelands and freshwater and marine habitats, the rate of destruction is increasing. This loss of habitat has resulted in declining numbers of many native species of animals and plants, some of which, like the Asian cheetah, are already extinct. In an effort to preserve wildlife and natural habitats, the government oversees an extensive national park and wildlife sanctuary system. The WWF recognizes fourteen national parks and ninety-nine wildlife sanctuaries in Pakistan, but the federation has stated that these sanctuaries are vulnerable to pressures caused by rapid population growth.

## POPULATION

Pakistan's population exceeds 140 million and is growing fast. Almost half of the population is under fifteen years of age, and the estimated annual growth rate of 3.0 percent is one of the highest of any developing country.

The major portion of Pakistan's population is concentrated in the fertile Indus River valley and along the river's major tributaries in the northern and northeastern portions of the country. By contrast, the western and southwestern areas of Pakistan are sparsely inhabited.

Widespread poverty persists in much of the population, particularly in the rural areas where two-thirds of Pakistanis live. At least 35 million people live in poverty, and public access to health, education, clean water, sanitation, and family planning remains low.

## PROVINCES

Pakistan is divided into four provinces: the North-West Frontier (usually referred to as NWFP), the Punjab, Sindh

(also spelled Sind), and Baluchistan (also spelled Beluchistan). In addition, there are several territories, including Azad Kashmir (the Pakistan-controlled portion of the disputed state of Jammu and Kashmir, often referred to simply as "Kashmir"), the Northern Areas, and a semiautonomous tribal area in the western border region.

*Farmers who grow crops on the steep slopes of the North-West Frontier province have to terrace the land.*

The North-West Frontier province runs for over 680 miles along the border with Afghanistan. The capital of the NWFP, Peshawar, is set in a wide, fertile valley that was the center of the ancient Buddhist kingdom of Gandhara. The northern half of the province consists of a series of parallel river valleys running approximately north and south. These valleys are on the northern edge of the monsoon belt, which allows them to be green in the southern sections while the more remote areas are essentially mountainous deserts. South of Peshawar, the NWFP consists of low, rocky mountains and wide plains of mostly gravel and sand. The NWFP contains large semiautonomous tribal areas that are outside the control of the Pakistani government, which makes this the oldest continuously lawless area in the world. The most powerful tribal people of the area are the Pashtuns (also spelled Pathans, Paktuns, or Pukhtuns), warriors who over the centuries have defeated the Moguls, Afghans, Sikhs, British, and Russians and continue to push for an independent Pashtun nation.

Baluchistan is the largest province of Pakistan, accounting for about 42 percent of the country's total land area. Known for its inhospitable Makran desert, Baluchistan is only sparsely inhabited. In fact, the population of Baluchistan accounts for only about 4 percent of the national total. Its biggest city, Quetta, is also the provincial capital. The northeastern border of Baluchistan is marked by the lofty Sulaiman Range, where the Khojak and Bolan Passes provide overland routes between the lower Indus valley and southern Afghanistan. Baluchistan is notorious for cross-border smuggling operations. It is a dangerous place where kidnapping for ransom is common. Almost every man in this region carries a gun, and shootings, armed robberies, and kidnappings are commonplace.

The Punjab is a densely populated and fertile region, and its major urban centers, especially Lahore, Islamabad, Rawalpindi, and Multan, have produced many of Pakistan's political and economic leaders. The name of this province is

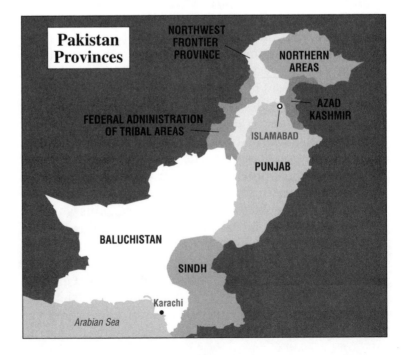

derived from the words *punj*, meaning "five", and *aab* meaning "waters", and the Punjab is crossed by five major rivers that all eventually flow into the Indus. These rivers make the Punjab excellent for farming, but they also make it an area that is often inundated by floods. When Pakistan gained its independence in 1947, the Punjab's eastern portion went to India but most of the state became part of Pakistan.

The Sindh province is bounded by the uninhabitable sands of the Thar Desert to the east, barren mountains to the west, and the Arabian Sea to the south. The capital is Karachi. The Indus plain running through the middle of the Sindh province is where civilization began in Pakistan. The water level of the Indus is often above the level of the surrounding plain, so embankments are required to prevent flooding, which nevertheless occurs frequently. The irrigated parts of Sindh are highly populated (about 20 million people in all), and although two-thirds of the population are employed in agriculture, electronics and other high-technology industries are growing rapidly. Hundreds of years ago, Sindh was called the Unhappy Valley because of its scorching deserts, dust, and hostile tribes, and today frequent assassinations, firefights, bombs, and murders make it an even more unpleasant place. Well-armed bandits are also common in Sindh, and they have been known to stop entire trains or vehicle caravans, often kidnapping and killing passengers.

## Major Cities

Islamabad, Pakistan's capital, is located in the Punjab near the foothills of the Himalayas. The design of Islamabad was laid out in the cool green hills north of Rawalpindi, and construction began in 1961. Today the capital is a clean city of wide, tree-lined avenues with sectors for government, commerce, residential, recreational, and industrial use. There are also sections of the city where no building may be built, and they form peaceful green parks. The population now stands at over half a million, yet traffic jams and pollution are rare due to good urban planning, effective public transportation, and a lack of heavy industry. Although crime plagues Pakistan's other major cities, Islamabad, the center of the country's government and the focus of foreign diplomatic missions, is still comparatively safe.

*Local children seem undaunted by Karachi's reputation as the most dangerous city in the world.*

Karachi, the capital of the Sindh province, is located on the Arabian Sea. A busy, polluted, and severely congested center of commerce and industry, Karachi is Pakistan's largest city with a population of almost 14 million. Karachi was Pakistan's original capital city but was replaced by Islamabad in the 1960s because it was considered too hot, too crowded, and too far away from Pakistan's ruling elite, who were mostly Punjabis. It is home to the country's only seaport, and its international airport is an important stop on east-west air routes. Some consider Karachi to be the most dangerous city in the world, and lurid reports of murders, bombings, robberies, and assassinations fill the newspapers every day. Although Karachi is the population center of southern Pakistan, Lahore in the northeastern part of the country is the second-largest city.

Lahore has a population of more than 6 million. It occupies a choice site in the midst of the Punjab's fertile plains not far from the Indian border. Retaining many remnants of its days as one of the most important cities of the Mogul empire, modern Lahore is regarded as the cultural, architectural, and artistic center of Pakistan.

In contrast, the city of Quetta is found on Pakistan's wild central frontier. Quetta is the capital of the province of Baluchistan and has a population of about half a million Pakistanis and a large number of Afghan refugees. Located near the Afghanistan border at an altitude of about fifty-five hundred feet, Quetta is an attractive mountain city known for its fruit orchards. Because of its strategic geographical position close to the southern Afghan city of Kandahar and the Bolan Pass, Quetta is both a border town and an important overland trade route. As a result, there is a major military presence here, a trait shared by both Quetta and Peshawar.

Peshawar is the capital of the North-West Frontier province and, with a population of almost a million people,

*Two armed Pakistani troopers in Quetta, a city that maintains a continual military presence because of its proximity to the Afghan border.*

it is the province's largest city. Peshawar has tremendous historical, military, and political importance because of its proximity to the Khyber Pass, the major overland route to the west. The city was founded over two thousand years ago, and through the centuries it has been a melting pot of civilizations. In the faces, languages, and clothing of the inhabitants, as well as in the city's architecture, can be seen evidence of the Mogul invaders, Chinese pilgrims, and Tajik traders who have ruled Peshawar. Old Peshawar is a true frontier town where groups of Pathan tribesmen stroll among the shops where gunsmiths make fully functional replicas of modern guns.

From Peshawar to Rawalpindi is a distance of only about one hundred miles, but the two cities are very different. Rawalpindi, usually called simply "Pindi" by Pakistanis, has a population of about 1.5 million. An important industrial and commercial center, the city has an oil refinery, gasworks, an iron foundry, railroad yards, a brewery, sawmills, and factories making tents, textiles, hosiery, pottery, and leather goods. Strategically located adjacent to the capital and on the road that links the Punjab to Kashmir, Rawalpindi is home to Pakistan's army headquarters. From 1959 to 1970, it was the interim capital of Pakistan. Rawalpindi is the industrial city of the north, and Hyderabad is its southern counterpart.

Hyderabad is a sprawling city of about 2 million people located on the banks of the Indus River in the Sindh province. It is one of the oldest cities of the subcontinent, with a history dating back to pre-Islamic times. Located on the edge of the Thar Desert, Hyderabad is very hot most of the year. For decades Hyderabad has been plagued by recurring outbreaks of ethnic and religious violence, and there have been numerous incidents of kidnapping for ransom.

Pakistan is geographically diverse with tall, glacier-clad mountains in the north, uninhabitable deserts in the west and east, a fertile central valley, and a long coast on the Arabian Sea. The urban centers range from clean, carefully planned modern communities to dangerous and desperate slum-filled cities. Rapid population growth endangers many aspects of Pakistani life, including wildlife, the environment, and efforts to reduce poverty and crime.

# Five Thousand Years of Civilization

The nation of Pakistan has existed only since 1947, but civilization in this part of the Indian subcontinent, which today includes Pakistan, India, and Bangladesh, dates back many millennia. During those thousands of years, the land that is modern Pakistan had been invaded many times. Consequently, a great variety of historical influences have contributed to the rich cultural mixture that makes up this diverse and intriguing country.

## The Indus Civilization

Archaeological evidence indicates that perhaps as early as fifty thousand years ago Stone Age tribes inhabited the fertile lands along the Indus River. By 7000 B.C. these primitive tribes had been replaced by humans who knew how to make tools and weapons from bronze. The first well-organized societies in Pakistan, however, appeared in the Indus valley about five thousand years ago.

Along ancient banks of the Indus are the remains of numerous complex and advanced cities, cities that were unknown to the modern world until first excavated during the 1920s. The Dravidians, a people whose roots are lost in history, built the first true civilization in the Indus valley. By 2000 B.C. they already possessed advanced agricultural practices, economic structures, mathematics, literature, and arts. Recent archaeological excavations have determined that the Indus civilization eventually grew to cover an area larger than Western Europe, much larger than contemporary civilizations along the Nile in Egypt and the Tigris-Euphrates region of Mesopotamia. The number of cities and villages belonging to the Indus civilization indicates its

*Dice found at Mohenjo Daro are thought to be four thousand to five thousand years old.*

enormity: 481 sites in Pakistan and 917 sites in northwestern India.

The most thoroughly studied of the ancient Dravidian cities are Mohenjo Daro and Harappa, both in the Indus valley. The ruins of these cities show they contained advanced street layouts and building designs. The uniformity of the two cities and other Dravidian centers suggests to archaeologists that this culture was united under a central government, although there is no evidence of what kind of government that might have been.

Mohenjo Daro's carefully laid-out streets, drainage systems, public baths, and grain storage facilities indicate to archaeologists that this may have been the earliest example of a planned city, a city that was designed to function efficiently rather than, like most ancient cities, simply growing as the population grew. Evidence unearthed there and elsewhere indicates that the Dravidians traded and exchanged ideas about religion, mathematics, and language with other civilizations to the west, including the Egyptians, Greeks, Babylonians, and Sumerians. The Dravidians kept records of their trading transactions and used written language with a distinctive script that had 419 symbols. Unfortunately, the early Dravidian script has never been deciphered. Today the descendants of the original Dravidians are relatively uncommon in Pakistan, but they make up a large percentage of the population in southern India.

### A SUCCESSION OF INVADERS

The Indus civilization of the Dravidians flourished for over a thousand years; then, in a relatively brief span of time, it disappeared. No one knows for sure what happened, although some believe that many years of drought or earthquakes contributed to the downfall. There is also some evidence that when Aryan nomads from central Asia began invading the subcontinent around 1800 B.C., they drove out the Dravidians. Whether it happened violently or peacefully, by 1500 B.C.

the lighter-skinned Aryans had replaced the dark-skinned Dravidians in what is now Pakistan and northern India, and the Dravidians had migrated to southern India.

The Aryans came to the subcontinent from the grasslands of central Asia. They were nomadic cattle herders who left very little behind to reveal their history: no cities, sculpture, pottery, or burial grounds have been found. The Aryans did, however, leave four books of verse called the Vedas, which provide the strongest evidence of their five-hundred-year domination of present-day Pakistan and India. Forming the foundations of modern Hinduism, the Vedas are a mixture of history and religious teachings. Filled with epic stories written mostly in verse, the Vedas tell about the way the Aryans lived and worshiped.

*Brick-edged drainage channels line a street in the ancient city of Mohenjo Daro.*

Following the Aryans, wave after wave of invaders from the west and north marched into the subcontinent. First came Darius I and his armies, who conquered the Aryans in 518 B.C. and added the Indus valley and part of the Punjab to the vast Persian Empire (centered in present-day Iran). From the Aryans Darius demanded and received immense wealth in the form of taxes. As a result, stories began to spread westward until word reached Europe about the great treasures to be found in the subcontinent.

In 327 B.C. the Greek warrior-king Alexander of Macedonia overthrew Darius III in Persia and continued eastward across present-day Afghanistan and through the mountain passes into what would one day be the Pakistani province of the Punjab. Alexander met determined resistance from the local people there, and he was soon forced to retreat by floating his army on rafts down the Indus River to the Arabian Sea.

After Alexander's departure, the area that would become Pakistan in the northwest sector of the subcontinent was

*A fragment of a centuries-old frieze from Taxila depicts Buddha and some of his followers.*

invaded repeatedly. Between the first and fifth centuries A.D., Buddhists settled the Taxila valley in the north of this region. The Buddhists and a series of Indian Hindu monarchs ruled the region for hundreds of years until they too

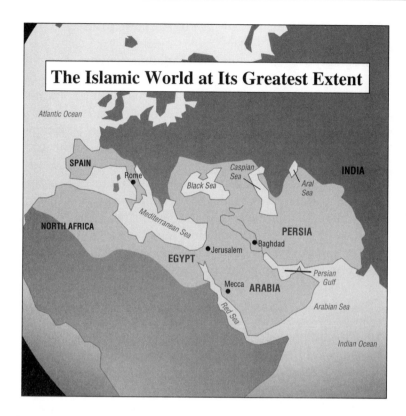

The Islamic World at Its Greatest Extent

succumbed to invaders, most notably the armies of a new religion, Islam.

## THE ARRIVAL OF ISLAM

The religion of Islam arose in the western Arabian Peninsula during the seventh century A.D. Muslims, as adherents to Islam are called, rapidly spread their new faith from southern Europe to India. The first Muslim army to reach the subcontinent was led by the Turkish sultan Mahmud, who plundered the Punjab over the course of several raids. He was not interested in conquering, and after a raid he returned through the Khyber Pass to his fortress in Ghazni (in present-day Afghanistan).

Following the Turkish raiders, in 644 an Arab Muslim army reached the province of Sindh in present-day Pakistan. By 711 Muslim Arabs had conquered Sindh and established deep Islamic roots there. The Arab warriors won converts by force, but the Islamic faith also appealed to low-caste and oppressed Hindus, so Muslims eventually became an increasingly important part of the subcontinent's cultural mosaic.

Gradually Muslim leaders succeeded in unifying much of the subcontinent, which led to almost five hundred years of unprecedented prosperity. But the riches of the subcontinent soon caught the eye of marauding Mongol Huns, warrior tribes from central Asia. One of the fiercest Mongol warlords was Timur the Lame (also called Tamerlane and Timer), who ransacked the northern capitals of the subcontinent in 1398. The attacks of the Huns also interrupted the essential trade routes across Asia and blocked the flow of goods that had made the subcontinent prosperous. Following the raids by the Mongol Huns, the entire region became a collection of small feuding kingdoms. This breakdown in unity opened the door for two new waves of invaders, one from the steppes of Asia, the other from Europe. The first to arrive were the Moguls.

## THE MOGUL PERIOD

Like the Mongol Huns to whom they were closely related, the Moguls (also spelled Moghuls or Mughals) came from central Asia and were great warriors; their goals were not to pillage and return home with the spoils, but to conquer and rule. In the process, they forever changed the cultures they conquered.

The first Mogul emperor, Babur, was a warrior in what is today southern Russia. Searching for glory and riches, he led his army through the Khyber Pass and, during the early 1500s, invaded what would one day be Pakistan. With ferocity and cunning backed by superior cavalry and artillery, by 1529 Babur had conquered most of the northern half of the subcontinent. The Mogul Empire was born.

After his death in 1530, Babur was followed by a succession of Mogul rulers, but Babur's grandson Akbar was by far the most influential of all. Akbar (reigned 1556–1605) came to the throne when he was only fourteen, but with the guidance of wise ministers he was able to gain full control of his empire while still a teenager. Under Akbar's tolerant and wise leadership, the Mogul Empire entered a period of peace and prosperity. Since the Moguls controlled the trade routes as well as major sources of spices, jewels, and many other riches, the Pakistani-Indian subcontinent became

# THE HISTORIC KHYBER PASS

The Khyber Pass is a thirty-three-mile-long passage winding through the Safed Koh mountains between Afghanistan and northwestern Pakistan. The pass, walled by precipitous cliffs that vary in height from about five hundred to nine hundred feet, reaches its highest elevation at the border between Afghanistan and Pakistan. At its narrowest point, the pass is only ten feet wide. The Khyber Pass is the best land route between India and Pakistan, and because of this, conquering armies have used the pass as an entry point for their invasions. It has also been a major trade route for centuries.

For hundreds of years, great camel caravans traveled through the Khyber Pass, bringing goods to trade. These ancient merchants carried silks and fine porcelain from China to the Middle East. Although the traders traveled in caravans, they were often robbed by local tribesmen when traveling through the Khyber Pass.

The Khyber Pass was also the scene of many battles, most notably between the British and Pashtun warriors during the nineteenth century. Many British soldiers are buried in the huge cemetery at the foot of the pass. The future prime minister of England, Winston Churchill, was wounded during a battle at the Khyber Pass.

Two highways thread their way through the Khyber Pass: one for motor traffic and one for camel caravans. A railroad (built between 1920 and 1925), which passes through thirty-four tunnels and over ninety-two bridges and culverts, runs to the Afghan border. Pakistan controls the entire pass. Since the 1980s and 1990s, the Khyber Pass has been used to transport refugees from the Afghan civil war into Pakistan and to transport arms into Afghanistan.

*Afghan refugees flee to neighboring Pakistan via the Khyber Pass.*

one of the richest and most powerful regions in the world. European countries became eager to establish friendly relations with the Mogul Empire, including the lands that would one day become Pakistan, to share in its fabulous wealth through trade.

After Akbar, the territory that was later to become much of present-day Pakistan and India was ruled by a succession of Mogul leaders. Aurangzeb (reigned 1658–1707) was the last strong Mogul emperor. He was a severe, humorless, devout Muslim who imposed extremely strict Islamic law on the subcontinent, imposed taxes that applied only to Hindus, and even persecuted other Muslims if they came from sects other than his own. His religious fanaticism led to widespread opposition and numerous rebellions. With enemies everywhere, he became so suspicious that he believed that members of his own family were plotting a rebellion, and he killed his own brothers and imprisoned his daughter and three sons.

A series of weak Mogul leaders followed Aurangzeb's death. Revolutions continually chipped away at the unity of the Mogul Empire until, bit by bit, Mogul power waned, paving the way for a new wave of foreigners, this time from Europe.

### THE BEGINNING OF BRITISH RULE

Even as the Moguls were building their empire on the subcontinent during the sixteenth century, the first Europeans began arriving. Gradually competition for the rich Mogul markets between traders from Portugal, France, Holland, and England became more intense. A long series of wars in Europe had nearly depleted many national treasuries, so it was inevitable that this competition would turn into violent conflicts. By 1700 the Europeans were fighting sea and land battles to gain control of access to the subcontinent's spices, fabrics, pearls, and other valuable commodities. Because of these battles, the European trading posts always included the presence of troops and warships, military forces that would eventually be turned on the local inhabitants themselves.

Representing English trading interests in the Mogul Empire, the British East India Company enjoyed the full military and political support of the British government without actually being controlled by the government. This company became the Mogul Empire's chief trading partner in return

for the British government's troops providing military assistance to the Moguls. The British thus found themselves fighting both their European enemies and the enemies of the Moguls on the subcontinent. The Moguls, who by this point were losing their grip on their empire, were becoming increasingly unable to enforce tax collection. The Mogul emperor saw the British, because of their military power, as the only means left to effectively collect taxes, so he authorized the British East India Company to collect taxes throughout the Mogul Empire. Great Britain saw this as an opportunity to become the dominant European power on the subcontinent, and seized it.

Back in England there was considerable support for stepping up military action and turning the subcontinent into a British colony. An influential segment of the British population felt a moral superiority to what it considered the "uncivilized" people of the world and looked at the subcontinent's non-Christians, tribal populations, uneducated peasants, Dravidians, and Aryans as incapable of self-government. To eighteenth-century England, British military control seemed the best way to spread "civilization" to these people and avoid chaos.

*The Mogul emperor grants the British governor of India the right to collect taxes throughout the empire.*

# KIPLING IN LAHORE

Rudyard Kipling, the English author of many well-known novels, poems, and stories and the 1907 Nobel Prize winner, was born in 1865 in Bombay, colonial India. He was sent to England for his education, and in 1882, when he was not yet seventeen, he sailed to India to join his parents, who were then living in the Islamic city of Lahore, a city that is now part of Pakistan.

Kipling worked as a newspaper journalist in Lahore for five years and three additional years in other parts of northern colonial India, and he learned a great deal about the people and places of the subcontinent. He would sometimes dress like the local people and, having acquired their languages and ways, travel unnoticed through the bazaars and villages. Encouraged by his editors to contribute his own impressions of colonial India, Kipling wrote numerous observant and witty articles. Many of his stories and poems were reissued in the form of inexpensive paperbacks suitable for reading on the train, which were called his Railway Library series. By the time Kipling was twenty-four, many British readers were calling him the best English writer in the colony.

As a result of his years in Lahore, many of Kipling's books and stories are set in and concerned with the area that became northern Pakistan. The stories he wrote during his last two years there were collected in *The Phantom Rickshaw*. This collection includes the story "The Man Who Would Be a King" about an English trader who sets himself up as a god and king of the Kalash people in the North-West Frontier province. Many of the poems, articles, and six volumes of collected short stories that were published in colonial India were reprinted in England, and when he returned to England in 1890, he was already an acclaimed writer.

*A water seller in Lahore, the city that was home to Rudyard Kipling for several years.*

By 1784 the situation on the subcontinent had become such a large economic and political issue in Great Britain that a special law, called the India Act, was passed. It placed the actions of the British East India Company under the direct control of the British government and paved the way for legalizing British control of the subcontinent. As a result, British military actions on the subcontinent became even more aggressive.

By 1818 the last armed resistance by Europeans and Indians to British control in most parts of the subcontinent had ended. The British East India Company had become the undisputed master of the regions that would become Pakistan and India. A diplomatic settlement that year formally installed British rule over much of the subcontinent, although the Baluchistan, Sindh, the Punjab, and the North-West Frontier province areas of present-day Pakistan continued to resist British rule for many more years.

The British finally succeeded in conquering the provinces of Sindh (in 1843) and the Punjab (in 1849), but total control was hindered by frequent and fierce attacks by Baluchi and Pashtun warriors from the mountains between present-day Pakistan and Afghanistan. The British occupied the Baluchi city of Quetta in 1876 but remained unsuccessful in their efforts to subdue the mountain warriors. In 1893 the British divided the Afghan region from the British-controlled areas in these mountains with a line from Chitral to Baluchistan, a line known as the Durand Line. The Durand Line forms the basis of the current boundary between Pakistan and Afghanistan.

The British were unable to subdue the tribes in the northwestern mountains, and in 1901 they finally gave up and created the semiautonomous North-West Frontier province. They encountered resistance from other tribal peoples in the area, and eventually realized they would one day have to grant independence to their huge colony. England therefore shifted from a policy of conquest to a policy of containment in an attempt to ease resistance to its rule.

## THE SEEDS OF MUSLIM NATIONALISM

At the start of the twentieth century, the British were the dominant power on the subcontinent. Both Hindus and Muslims were dissatisfied under British rule and were beginning to agitate for independence. Muslims and Hindus both pressed the independence issue and formally created the Indian National Congress (INC) in 1885, which became the strongest representative of their various independence movements. The INC attempted to unite, at the national level, all of the different groups in the subcontinent that were pressing for independence and to present a strong political organization that the British could not ignore. The British were finding it increasingly difficult and expensive to maintain their control over the subcontinent's restless millions. As they explored ways to grant independence to their immense colony, the INC was anxious to become the people's representative on the path toward independence.

At first, Congress, as the INC became known, included members of both religions and strongly favored a single Indian nation that included people of all religions. But since Hindus far outnumbered Muslims on the subcontinent, Congress was always dominated by the Hindus, and most Muslims deeply feared that Hindus would dominate independent India. As a result Muslim leaders began to speak of two separate countries, sowing the seeds of the Two Nations Theory. This notion called for separate Muslim and Hindu nations and led to the formation in 1906 of the All-India Muslim League.

The primary goal of the Muslim League was to advance the cause of a separate country that would be headed by Muslims. To build momentum toward a separate Islamic country, the league urged the subcontinent's Muslims to gain political power and keep their sense of Muslim identity. The most stalwart promoter of this idea for a separate nation for Muslims was Mohammed Ali Jinnah, called "the Father of Pakistan."

Jinnah was an early member of Congress and an enthusiastic supporter of India's struggle for independence from British rule. As a Muslim, he also joined the Muslim League in 1913, and for six years he was a member of both Congress and the Muslim League. As a vocal member and supporter of both parties, he became known as an ambassador of Hindu-Muslim unity. But that was not to last.

During World War I Britain used Indian soldiers, both Hindu and Muslim, in its armies. At first both the Muslims and Hindus begrudgingly supported the British war effort.

# JINNAH, THE FATHER OF PAKISTAN

For Pakistanis, Mohammad Ali Jinnah is the *Quaid-e-Azam*, or "Great Leader." A British-educated lawyer, he became the leader of the struggle for a Muslim nation as the subcontinent negotiated its independence from Britain. Relentless in his insistence on partition—meaning separate Muslim and Hindu states—Jinnah was a complex man who inspired both praise and condemnation.

Jinnah was born in 1876 in Karachi, at that time part of British India. The son of a wealthy merchant, his family could afford to send him to England where he studied law; at age nineteen he became the youngest Indian ever to pass the British bar (law exam). He returned to India in 1896, where he quickly became a prominent and respected lawyer.

Jinnah soon entered politics and became passionately committed to achieving independence from England. Worried that British oppression of all Indians would be replaced by Hindu oppression of the Muslim minority, Jinnah gradually began to advocate a separate state for Muslims.

His dream came true in 1947, and Jinnah became governor-general of the new Muslim nation of Pakistan. But Jinnah did not live to see the development of the new country. He died of tuberculosis just thirteen months after the formation of Pakistan.

Jinnah's contribution to history was summed up by biographer Stanley Wolpert in his book *Jinnah of Pakistan*: "Few individuals significantly alter the course of history. Fewer still modify the map of the world. Hardly anyone can be credited with creating a nation-state. Mohammad Ali Jinnah did all three."

*Mohammad Ali Jinnah, the founder and first governor-general of Pakistan.*

However, at that time the Ottoman Empire was the center of authority for the Islamic world, and the British were at war with the Ottomans. As British forces attacked and defeated the Muslim Ottoman armies, Indian Muslims became increasingly antagonistic toward the British. As Muslims and Hindus split over support for the British war effort, the gulf between Congress and the Muslim League widened, and Jinnah divorced himself from Congress.

After World War I ended the British resumed efforts toward creating an independent India. With Jinnah no longer in Congress, however, Muslims and Hindus disagreed on virtually every point pertaining to independence. Congress had made considerable progress in convincing the British that a single India was the only way to have stability after independence, but the Muslim League absolutely refused to consider an independence that did not allow for a separate Muslim state. The British were beginning to doubt they could ever achieve a peaceful independence for the Hindus and Muslims of the subcontinent.

Gradually, however, the tide of British opinion began to turn, influenced in part by the eloquent words of Sir Muhammad Iqbal, a poet, lawyer, and the subcontinent's leading Muslim philosopher. In 1930 the British listened as Iqbal demanded "the formation of a consolidated Muslim state in the best interests of India and Islam. For India, it means security and peace resulting from an internal balance of power; for Islam, an opportunity . . . to mobilize its laws, its education, its culture, and to bring them into closer contact with its own original spirit and with the spirit of modern times."[1]

Iqbal went on to describe the specific boundaries he envisioned for the Muslim state. His proposed boundaries were almost identical to modern Pakistan, although the name *Pakistan* did not yet exist.

### PAKISTAN'S NAME

In 1933 a Pakistani law student at England's Cambridge University, Rahmat Ali, played an important role in Pakistan's history. While in Great Britain, Ali founded an organization, the Pakistan National Movement, to publicize the cause of a separate Muslim state in India after independence. He also coined the name *Pakistan* in a pamphlet he wrote titled "Now or Never."

Ali created the name *Pakistan* from the letters of the areas in and around the future nation: *P* for Punjab, *A* for Afghania, *K* for Kashmir, *I* to ease pronunciation, *S* for Sindh, and *TAN* (meaning "land of") from the last syllable of Afghanistan, Baluchistan, and Turkharistan. In addition, *pak* means "pure and clean" in Urdu, the language spoken in much of northern Pakistan.

In his pamphlet "Now or Never," Ali made one of the clearest statements for the establishment of an independent Muslim nation on the subcontinent when he wrote,

> India, constituted as it is at the present moment, is not the name of one single country; nor the home of one single nation. . . . In the five Northern Provinces of India, out of a total population of about forty millions, we, the Muslims, contribute about 30 millions. Our religion, culture, history, tradition, economic system, laws of inheritance, succession and marriage are basically and fundamentally different from those of the people living in the rest of India. The ideals which move our thirty million brethren-in-faith living in these provinces to make the highest sacrifices are fundamentally different from those which inspire the Hindus. These differences are not confined to the broad basic principles—far from it. They extend to the minutest details of our lives. We do not inter-dine; we do not inter-marry. Our national customs, calendars, even our diet and dress are different.[2]

Ali's group and the Muslim League lobbied extensively in Britain to continue turning public opinion in favor of their cause, and they had considerable success. As independence loomed, the Muslim League was confident that it would soon have its separate nation, but World War II postponed independence again, as it drew Britain's attention away from the independence issue.

## THE FINAL STEPS

At the annual meeting of the Muslim League in Lahore in 1940, Jinnah told the world that the goal of a separate Muslim state is

> based on the fundamental principle that the Muslims of India are an independent nationality and any attempt to get them to merge their national and political identity

and unity will not only be resisted but, in my opinion, it will be futile for anyone to attempt it. We are determined, and let there be no mistake about it, to establish the status of an independent State in this subcontinent.[3]

At that meeting, the Muslim League made its final plan for partition, as the division of the subcontinent into separate Hindu and Muslim states came to be known. The league decided that the areas of northwestern and eastern India, where Muslims were in the majority, should form the basis of a two-part Muslim nation, laying the foundation of modern Pakistan. This plan became known as the Lahore Resolution, later called the Pakistan Resolution although the word *Pakistan* did not appear in it initially. Congress, however, stridently opposed the Lahore Resolution, but as far as the Muslim League was concerned the stage was set for independence and partition following the end of the war.

### AFTER WORLD WAR II

When World War II ended in 1945, independence for colonial India once again became a pressing topic in both England and the subcontinent. The first postwar elections on the subcontinent revealed that the people were, as many feared, split on purely religious grounds. The Muslim League, led by Jinnah, represented Muslims, and Congress, led by Jawaharlal Nehru, represented Hindus. Early in 1946 a British mission attempted one last time to negotiate an agreement between the two sides that would allow them to live together in one united country. The talks failed, and the subcontinent slid ever closer to war between Muslims and Hindus. Then, in 1947, the Muslim League called for a "direct action" day in which Muslims throughout the subcontinent were to demonstrate in favor of partition. A demonstration in Calcutta, however, deteriorated into a slaughter of Hindus at the hands of a rampaging Muslim mob. The Hindus responded with deadly reprisals against Muslims in many parts of the country. It took a month for the bloodshed to finally stop.

Reluctantly, the British made the decision to divide India. They agreed to follow essentially the plan for partition proposed by the Muslim League in its Lahore Resolution. The new Muslim nation of Pakistan was to consist of two parts

*A 1947 Muslim League protest attracted thousands. The day ended in disaster as Muslims slaughtered Hindus.*

separated by the vast bulk of mostly Hindu India. This unusual arrangement was deemed necessary because although some areas were clearly Hindu and others clearly Muslim, the main Muslim areas were on extreme opposite ends of the subcontinent. East Pakistan would occupy the northeastern part of the former colony, and West Pakistan would occupy the northwestern part. Travel between the eastern and western parts of Pakistan would have to pass through India.

The picture was further complicated by the fact that many areas within what would soon be independent India had evenly mixed populations of both religions while other areas had isolated populations of Muslims surrounded by Hindus. Muslims who lived there before partition had the choice of staying or moving to Pakistan. The impossibility of separating all Muslims from all Hindus was illustrated by the fact that even after colonial India was partitioned, India was and still is the third-largest Muslim country in the world!

## INDEPENDENCE AND THE FIRST WAR WITH INDIA

Once the awkward division was decided upon, a democratic parliamentary system of government was established for both Pakistan and India, and interim leaders were selected until elections could be organized, the British moved quickly. At midnight on August 14, 1947, the British relinquished their control over the subcontinent, and Pakistan and India finally became independent nations.

# 3

# A Troubled Independence

As the Muslims of colonial India celebrated their independence, several circumstances put the fledgling nation on a path toward a long series of troubles. Although the newly formed nation was overwhelmingly Muslim, it consisted of many culturally distinct peoples with divergent and often conflicting interests, a situation that caused internal problems from independence until the present. Furthermore, major points of disagreement between India and Pakistan remained unsettled by the provisions of independence, which led to a number of wars and skirmishes between the two neighbors. These manmade problems combined with a string of natural disasters to hamper Pakistan's development from the beginning.

### Immediate Chaos

For several months after Pakistan and India were officially split into two independent nations, tens of millions of people moved east and west across the subcontinent as Muslims living in India left for Pakistan and Hindus and Sikhs (many of whom lived in the Punjab, most of which was now part of Pakistan) living in Pakistan moved to India. Political leaders on both sides, seeking to gain an advantage for the upcoming elections, fanned the fears of the masses with stories of theft and atrocities committed by the other side. Even though most of the stories proved to be false, trainloads of Muslims leaving India for Pakistan were held up and slaughtered by Hindu and Sikh mobs while Hindus and Sikhs traveling in the other direction suffered the same fate at the hands of Muslim mobs. In the Punjab alone, during the first three months after independence almost half a mil-

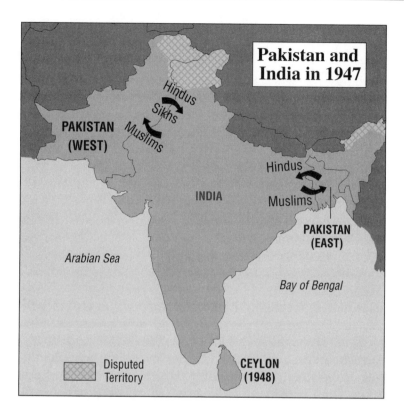

lion people lost their lives as they attempted to move from one new nation to the other.

The division of Pakistan into eastern and western parts caused problems from the start. Although most of the country's political parties had branches in both the east and the west, West Pakistanis held the real power. The Bengali people, who constituted the majority of East Pakistanis, felt the political leaders were failing to protect their interests at the national level. The West Pakistanis and the Bengalis were both Muslim, but they differed greatly in language, culture, and ethnicity. Consequently, in 1949 frustrated Bengalis created the Awami League to promote their interests. The Awami League quickly became the leading party of East Pakistan and immediately began pressing for the independence of East Pakistan.

Another problem created during partition was the failure of the British to settle the issue of whether India or Pakistan would get the state of Jammu and Kashmir located in the highlands between the two new countries. Kashmir, as the

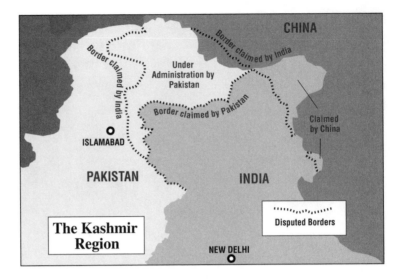

The Kashmir Region

state was often called, had a population that was mostly Muslim, but the local ruler was Hindu, and the British left it up to this ruler, the maharaja of Jammu and Kashmir, to decide whether to merge with Pakistan or India. The maharaja was indecisive: A month after partition, he still had not made a choice. Muslim tribesmen from Pakistan's North-West Frontier province decided that Jammu and Kashmir should go to Pakistan since it was mostly Muslim. In September 1947 a large band of armed tribesmen entered Jammu and Kashmir from Pakistan. Fearing for his life, the maharaja asked India for help, which India provided under the condition that Jammu and Kashmir become part of India. The maharaja agreed, and in October 1947 Indian troops arrived and quickly took control of more than half the state, claiming it for India. The Pakistani government refused to recognize the maharaja's decision, claimed Jammu and Kashmir as Pakistani territory, and sent troops from their own brand-new army into the region. Only a few months after partition Pakistan and India fought their first war, which lasted well into 1948. India finally defeated Pakistan, gaining control of the eastern two-thirds of Jammu and Kashmir while Pakistan gained the western third.

## THE CHALLENGE OF PAKISTANI LEADERSHIP

In 1948, a little more than a year after independence and partition, Pakistan's founder and first ruler, Mohammed Ali

Jinnah, died. His death robbed Pakistanis of the man who, more than any other, had inspired the creation of their nation.

The loss of Jinnah left Pakistan without a strong leader, and the failure to wrest Kashmir from India left the country feeling vulnerable in the face of its more powerful neighbor. Pakistan quickly moved to build up its army, but without simultaneously strengthening other parts of the country, economic conditions deteriorated. Dissatisfaction with the government's failure to address high unemployment and stabilize the economy led to widespread rioting. Several government figures, including the prime minister, were assassinated. To quell the unrest, in 1953 the army took over the government and imposed martial law. This marked the beginning of a pattern that was to characterize Pakistan's government throughout the first five decades of its existence. Elected leaders would turn out to be weak or corrupt, economic and social problems would escalate until the army stepped in, and a military dictatorship would run the country until eventually the military would allow elections. Then the cycle would start again.

Upon gaining independence, Pakistan adopted a temporary parliamentary form of government with the expectation that the country's leaders would soon write a constitution protecting the rights of the citizens and spelling out the structure of the government. The creation of a constitution, however, was repeatedly postponed while the military government dealt with assassinations, civil unrest, military coups, and war with India. Finally in 1956, in an effort to create a lasting governmental structure that would eliminate the need for military intervention, the military government allowed elections and the creation of the country's first constitution.

Several short-lived civil governments came and went under the constitution of 1956. Pakistan was discovering that the Muslim faith was not enough to keep disagreements between the country's bickering tribal and regional groups from deteriorating into riots and violence. Elected leaders tended to be corrupt and often ignored the needs of everyone other than their own supporters, which left the rest of the population disgruntled. It seemed that only the army could prevent the corruption and outbreaks of violence that haunted Pakistan's elected governments. Before the end of the 1950s the army took over again, placing the country under the dictatorship of General Mohammad Ayub Khan.

## MORE GENERALS, MORE WAR

For almost eight years Ayub Khan ruled both the country and the armed forces. He diverted more funds to the army and continued the military buildup that had started soon after partition. By 1965 the army felt it was strong enough to once again challenge India over the unresolved issue of Jammu and Kashmir, and Ayub Khan led the country into its second war with India. Fighting in the high altitudes and cold climate of the Kashmir mountains, the Indians proved to be stronger than the Pakistani forces and easily defeated the Pakistani army. Pakistan's loss to India in its second war over Kashmir disgraced Ayub Khan, and massive demonstrations against his regime continued for years until he was forced to resign in 1969.

*General Mohammad Ayub Khan addresses reporters in London in 1968.*

Ayub Khan was succeeded by another general, Yahya Khan. He had moderate success in restoring calm to Pakistan, but he too focused more on strengthening the military instead of attending to pressing domestic issues. One of those issues, one that had begun during Ayub Khan's reign, was about to literally tear the country apart.

## East Pakistan Secedes

From the moment of independence, East Pakistan was dissatisfied with the government. East Pakistanis complained that because the country's political, military, and economic controls were all centered in West Pakistan, particularly in Sindh and the Punjab, the west had unfair influence over the entire country. To make matters worse, the government had imposed Urdu, the language of upper-class Punjabis, as the country's official language, even though only 10 percent of all Pakistanis and less than 1 percent of East Pakistanis spoke the language.

The Awami League, which represented the Bengalis of East Pakistan, increasingly threatened to break from West Pakistan. Not surprisingly, the league's agenda was not well received in West Pakistan. The president of the Awami League and leader of the independent East Pakistan movement, Sheikh Mujibur Rahman (known simply as "Mujib"), was arrested in 1966 and imprisoned for his political activities. This only widened the gulf between West and East Pakistan.

Despite the fact that Mujib had been in prison and unable to campaign, in the elections of December 1970 the Awami League emerged as the largest political party in all of Pakistan. The next largest party, Zulfikar Ali Bhutto's Pakistan People's Party (PPP), emerged with a majority only in West Pakistan. The Awami League demanded and received Mujib's release from prison and forced the second-place PPP to open talks with them about the division of power between the parties and ultimately the independence of East Pakistan.

At this point, however, Pakistan was still firmly in the grip of General Yahya Khan, who had no intention of allowing the Awami League to achieve its most cherished goal, the independence of East Pakistan. On March 1, 1971, the general indefinitely postponed the pending National Assembly session at which the topic of East Pakistan's independence was to be discussed. The Awami League responded by calling

*Sheikh Mujibur Rahman gives a press conference in a London hotel after his release from prison in 1972.*

for massive strikes and civil disobedience in East Pakistan. Yahya Khan sent large numbers of troops into Dhaka, the capital of East Pakistan, arrested Mujib again, and outlawed the Awami League. Fearing arrest, the remaining Awami League leaders fled to India, where they organized a provisional government in exile.

Millions of Bengalis fled from East Pakistan into India to escape Yahya Khan's army as it attempted to suppress the independence movement. India decided to support the goals of the Awami League, which aggravated tensions between India and Pakistan. Finally, in December 1971, India invaded East Pakistan to fight Yahya Khan's army on behalf of the East Pakistanis, plunging the two countries into their third war with each other since independence. The Indian army moved swiftly and within ten days had captured Dhaka and forced the army of West Pakistan to surrender. Mujib was freed from prison, and soon after his release East Pakistan declared itself independent. The new country took the name of Bangladesh, meaning "Home of the Bengalis."

## ZULFIKAR ALI BHUTTO AND A NEW CONSTITUTION

Another defeat at the hands of the Indian army and the loss of the eastern half of the country temporarily threw West

Pakistan, now simply called Pakistan, into disarray. On almost the last day of 1971 Yahya Khan was forced to resign in the face of a huge public outcry against him. He was replaced by his foreign minister, the popular liberal Punjabi Zulfikar Ali Bhutto, the head of the PPP. Bhutto became president with the country still under martial law and no constitution in place.

Bhutto acted decisively to restore national confidence, quickly taking steps to strengthen the economy, attract foreign investors, and modernize the major industries and banking system. In 1973 he pushed through a new constitution that was accepted by most of the country's political elements. He called for free elections and was elected prime minister.

At first Bhutto's government looked like it might be different than Pakistan's previous elected governments, but soon charges of corruption began weakening his grip on power. Then, in 1977, his party was accused of election fraud, and violent demonstrations wracked the country. Again the military stepped in, arresting Bhutto and other leaders, suspending most of the 1973 constitution, postponing elections, and installing General Mohammad Zia-ul-Haq as president.

## Zia-ul-Haq's Legacy of Islamization

Zia-ul-Haq launched criminal investigations of the previous government that led to charges against Bhutto of conspiring to murder a political opponent. Bhutto was subsequently convicted and sentenced to death. Despite international appeals on his behalf, Bhutto was hanged on April 6, 1979. Zia-ul-Haq then set about building support for his own regime.

Zia-ul-Haq was a devout Muslim who believed that a secular Muslim state as envisioned by Mohammed Ali Jinnah, the country's founder, was a contradiction in terms. Zia-ul-Haq believed that Pakistan should become a more Islamic republic by installing religious law, called *Shari'a*, as the highest law of the nation. He found support for his plan in the country's religious scholars, but he needed the backing of the army too. Zia-ul-Haq began replacing moderate military leaders with generals who were sympathetic to Islamic fundamentalism. With the military and Muslim clergy firmly behind him, Zia-ul-Haq replaced most of the country's existing civil laws with strict Islamic law.

In his Islamization program, Zia-ul-Haq created one particularly far-reaching change in the country. Urged by his strongest political allies, the Islamic clergy, he encouraged the development of thousands of *madrassas*, or religious schools. Filled with Pakistan's impoverished young men, the *madrassas* fell under the control of militant Muslim extremists who used them to build the Taliban movement that would eventually rule Afghanistan.

By 1988 Zia-ul-Haq headed an army that was controlled by officers loyal to him and who, for the most part, brought a strict Islamic approach to their duties. Zia-ul-Haq had also introduced other laws that effectively prevented his opponents from running for office if he ever allowed elections. It seemed that Zia-ul-Haq was well positioned to rule Pakistan until his death.

Then, in August 1988, a plane carrying Zia-ul-Haq, the American ambassador to Pakistan, an American general,

*Two years after his installation as president, Mohammad Zia-ul-Haq set about turning Pakistan into a fundamentalist Islamic republic.*

and twenty-eight of Zia-ul-Haq's top military officers crashed, killing all of its occupants. In accordance with what remained of the 1973 constitution, the chairman of the Senate became acting president. He immediately announced that the elections would take place within months, and those elections would not be hampered by Zia-ul-Haq's legal restrictions.

## A Return to Elected Government

Despite the fact that former prime minister Bhutto had been hanged, the remnants of his political party, the Pakistan People's Party (PPP), put together a winning candidate in the coming elections. Bhutto's daughter, Benazir Bhutto, possessed her father's political skills and connections and became leader of the PPP after his death. The PPP succeeded in the 1988 elections, and she became prime minister, the first female leader of a Muslim country in modern times.

Unfortunately, the country was divided into numerous factions, preventing Bhutto and the PPP from governing effectively. As a result, many social and economic programs that could have benefited Pakistan were not enacted. Furthermore, Bhutto and her government became embroiled in scandal and corruption, and although she was prime minister, law and order in Pakistan deteriorated once again.

Throughout most of the 1990s, control of the government went back and forth between the PPP and a coalition of Islamic parties loyal to the Zia-ul-Haq tradition. Then, in 1998, prime minister Nawaz Sharif, a member of the Pakistan Muslim League, approved an event that would shock the world.

## Pakistan Gets the Atom Bomb

On May 28, 1998, Pakistan successfully exploded six atomic bombs in nuclear tests conducted in a remote location in the province of Baluchistan. The tests were Pakistan's direct response to India's five nuclear explosions just two weeks earlier. A nuclear war between Pakistan and India was now possible, and this realization stunned and frightened the rest of the world.

After the Pakistani and Indian atomic bomb tests, the United Nations Security Council unanimously passed a

# THE FIRST WOMAN OF ISLAMIC POLITICS

Benazir Bhutto, the eldest child of Pakistani prime minister Zulfikar Ali Bhutto, was born on June 21, 1953, in Karachi. After graduating from Harvard's Radcliffe University with a degree in political science in 1973, she attended Oxford University in England, where she completed graduate work in politics, philosophy, and economics. In 1977 Bhutto returned to Pakistan, where she assisted her father as an adviser.

Shortly after Bhutto's return to her homeland, her life turned tragic. Her father's head of the army, General Mohammad Zia-ul-Haq, overthrew the government, imprisoned her father, and declared martial law. Zia-ul-Haq also imprisoned Benazir Bhutto for five years, including ten months in solitary confinement. While she was in prison, the Zia-ul-Haq regime executed her father for conspiring to murder an opponent. When she was finally released, Zia-ul-Haq sent her into exile in England, where she lived for two years.

In 1986 Zia-ul-Haq allowed Bhutto to return to Pakistan. She was welcomed by huge crowds everywhere she went, partially because she was now head of the popular Pakistan People's Party and partially because she was the daughter of the beloved former prime minister. When Zia-ul-Haq died in an airplane crash in 1988, the Supreme Court of Pakistan allowed elections and Benazir Bhutto was chosen to lead the country. She became the first female prime minister of Pakistan on December 1, 1988.

Her first three years as prime minister ended with charges of corruption, but she returned a few years later and was appointed prime minister a second time. After three more years she was once again dismissed on grounds of corruption, as her husband and father-in-law were jailed for drug trafficking. Today she once again lives in exile in England, bitter about her failure to accomplish much for her country.

*Benazir Bhutto became the first female prime minister of Pakistan in 1988.*

resolution requiring both nations to halt their nuclear weapons programs. The United States and other countries imposed damaging economic sanctions against Pakistan and India until they agreed to stop nuclear testing, and the United Nations urged both countries to sign the Comprehensive Test Ban Treaty (CTBT), pledging to cease all nuclear testing.

Both sides said that they had finished their nuclear tests. In June 1998 Pakistan offered to join in new peace talks with India and proposed a nuclear weapon–free zone in south Asia. Pakistan also offered to sign the CTBT, provided India simultaneously did the same. As of March 2002, neither nation had signed the treaty.

## ANOTHER WAR OVER KASHMIR

Having the bomb, however, did little to help Pakistan's economic woes and civil unrest. Sharif's government attempted to improve Pakistan's economic troubles, but widespread corruption, an outbreak of terrible violence between different Muslim sects, and a prolonged fight over appointments of Supreme Court judges distracted the government. Then, in 1999, another confrontation between Pakistani and Indian soldiers along the Line of Control in Kashmir resulted in an undeclared war, and the world held its breath wondering if the conflict would escalate into a nuclear war. No nuclear bombs were unleashed by either side, and the confrontation ended with no change in the boundaries of Kashmir.

Following the inconclusive 1999 conflict with India, Sharif tried to push through a highly unpopular tax increase. With the prospect of a new tax, violence between rival sects still sweeping the country, and no real accomplishments to show for his leadership, Pakistanis were ready for new leadership, and found it in typical Pakistani fashion. After investigations suggested that Sharif had stolen over a billion dollars from the country, General Pervez Musharraf, the chief of the armed forces, seized power on October 12, 1999.

## MILITARY RULE AGAIN

Musharraf promised that the country would return to free elections and full democracy as soon as Pakistan became more politically and economically stable. Until that time, Musharraf declared himself to be the ruler of Pakistan and suspended the National Assembly and the constitution.

## MODERN MUSHARRAF

General Pervez Musharraf, the president of Pakistan since 1999, is an enigma. Pakistan's large middle class, hungry for anything that symbolizes modern global values, is fascinated by Musharraf, who somehow manages to be a military dictator while at the same time embodying modernity. He openly flaunts traditional Islamic taboos with his pet dogs (considered dirty by conservative Muslims) and consumption of alcohol. And he often wears Armani suits (like many other popular clothing brands, Armani suits are assembled in Pakistan for export, and therefore are not very expensive), plays golf, canoes, and sails.

Musharraf and his family live modestly, particularly compared to his almost universally corrupt predecessors, and they fully embrace the freedoms of modern living. The Musharrafs encouraged their eldest daughter, Ayla, to attend college. In college, she studied architecture, which is an unconventional field for a Pakistani woman, and she even dated. Ayla eventually married a man in a "love" marriage, as opposed to the more traditional "arranged" marriage. Her parents not only fully approved of the marriage, but they also broke another Pakistani traditional taboo by allowing Ayla to marry a man from a different Muslim sect than her own.

It should come as no surprise then that Musharraf has earned himself many enemies. Even though he has promised to hold democratic elections as soon as the country is more stable, many who have come to view Musharraf as the voice of reason in a country with such a history of extremism and corruption worry that his conservative enemies may find a way to end his reign.

*General Pervez Musharraf maintains a moderate and stable regime.*

Although some Western observers saw the latest military coup in Pakistan as a turn for the worse, most Pakistanis saw it as a positive development in a country where elected officials have consistently proven to be corrupt and oppressive. Under Musharraf, the media were freer than they were under the elected government of Sharif, whose aides frequently intimidated journalists. Pakistanis saw Musharraf as a liberal-minded modernizer who shakes hands with women in full public view (a rarity in conservative Muslim cultures), speaks with conviction about economic and social reforms, and, despite being a dictator, promotes human rights more effectively than the officials of recent democratic governments. And unlike previous anticorruption drives in Pakistan's history, Musharraf targeted officials from all political parties and ethnic groups.

In late 2001, following the September 11 terrorist attacks on the United States, Musharraf decided to support the Americans in their fight against the Taliban government of Afghanistan. He did so against the wishes of much of the Pakistani population, particularly the country's radical Islamic groups. After ten years of pro-Taliban activity in Pakistan, Musharraf knew he would have to act decisively to prevent a coup or revolution led by Islamic extremists. Ignoring the demands of the radicals, he removed leading pro-Taliban generals, placed top-level pro-Taliban religious leaders under house arrest, and closed the offices of radical Islamic organizations.

Musharraf, one of the last Western-educated officers left in the Pakistani army after Zia-ul-Haq's Islamization of the military, found himself in the middle of two opposing forces. With the West, especially the United States, and Islamic militants making opposite demands on him, Musharraf's success or failure in handling his polarized country could determine which of two very different paths Pakistan will take in the years to come.

# 4

# Everyday Life in Pakistan

Although Pakistan is ethnically diverse, the people are over-whelmingly Muslim. Islam is the force that unites the country. A majority of Pakistanis are members of tribal societies that dwell in rural settings, but tens of millions of people also live in giant cities like Karachi, which are filled with the same kinds of social challenges faced by other urbanized nations. But whether it is Pakistan's tribal or urban societies, the key to understanding most of the country's strengths and struggles lies in its Islamic culture.

## A Nation of Tribes

A Pakistani's position in society is determined by tribal affiliations and family ties. In rural Pakistan, where the majority of Pakistanis live, tribal life is the main form of society, and even in the cities tribal loyalties often affect social and business connections. In areas ruled by tribal traditions, especially in the borderlands near Afghanistan and in the North-West Frontier province, the people give tribal traditions precedence over any laws that come from the capital, Islamabad.

The majority of Pakistan's tribesmen make their living by farming and raising livestock, but many are nomadic herdsmen and caravaners who sometimes smuggle weapons and drugs. Despite these characteristics shared by most of Pakistan's tribes, they also differ from one another in many ways. Most tribes have their own language, which often prevents social and business interactions between different tribes and frustrates the government's efforts to unite Pakistani society. Islam helps to knit the disparate tribes together, but even here traces of various pre-Islamic beliefs linger. Some tribes still believe that there is an unseen world of gods, demons, fairies, and ancestral spirits, and others depend on shamans (priests or priestesses) to cure the sick by magic, communicate with the gods, and control events.

The North-West Frontier is closely identified with Pashtuns, one of the largest tribal groups in the world. The Pashtuns are also the dominant tribal group in the province of Baluchistan and the major tribe in southern Afghanistan, just across the border. The Pashtuns are fiercely independent and continuously agitate for their own nation.

There are more than 14 million Pashtuns in Pakistan, considerably more than in Afghanistan, and they make up the majority of the population north of Quetta between the Sulaiman Range and the Indus River. The greater Pashtun tribe is divided into about sixty tribes of varying size and importance, each of which occupies a specific territory.

*A Pashtun man grooms his beard before opening his shop in downtown Peshawar.*

Pashtuns live by a male-centered code of conduct, called the *pashtunwali*, which is basically the Pashtun interpretation of Islamic teachings. The most important concept of *pashtunwali* is honor, which Pashtun men view as being an all-or-nothing concept. Without honor, life for a Pashtun is not worth living. Pashtun honor means that a man must, at all costs, preserve the purity and reputations of his mother, daughters, sisters, and wife. Consequently, most Pashtun men keep their women in private family compounds. Furthermore, offenses to a Pashtun man's honor must be avenged. As a result, vendettas and feuds are a common feature of Pashtun society.

*Pashtunwali* is more than vendettas and feuds, however. Pashtuns take hospitality very seriously, using it to show respect, friendship, and alliance. Complex prescribed behaviors surround the serving of guests, in which the host or his sons refuse to sit with those they entertain as a

mark of courtesy. Pashtuns will give refuge to anyone, even an enemy, if that person is inside the grounds of the Pashtun's home, and for a Pashtun, refuge includes being willing to sacrifice your own life to defend your guest.

After the Pashtuns, the Bughtis are one of the oldest and largest tribes in Pakistan. The Bughtis, who also live near the Afghan border, are an extremely independent tribe with their own language and laws. They are warlike nomads who live as they have lived for centuries, crossing borders at will, making many of their own clothes, tending their herds, and using candlelight and campfires at night. Almost every one of Pakistan's 187,000 Bughti tribesmen are armed, and automatic weapons and rocket launchers are common possessions.

The Bughtis exemplify the tribal spirit of independence. According to Carol Lin, a reporter for CNN who stayed with the Bughtis in Pakistan, "The tribal chief . . . leads his elders in a series of meetings every day seven days a week, where it is the tribal elders and the chief—not the Pakistani government or the Pakistani police—who determine the laws of the land when it comes to the Bughti tribe."[4]

### THE LANGUAGES OF PAKISTAN

More than twenty languages are spoken in Pakistan, the most common of which are Punjabi, Sindhi, Urdu, Pashto, and Baluchi. Punjabi is spoken by about half of all Pakistanis. Reflecting England's long presence on the subcontinent, about 8 percent of Pakistanis speak English. That is about the same percentage as those who speak Urdu, the country's official language. Many educated and upwardly mobile Pakistanis speak Urdu or English in their homes.

The two strongest modern influences on Pakistan's languages are India, because both countries speak languages with Dravidian and Aryan roots, and the Middle East, because the script and vocabulary of Pakistani languages have borrowed heavily from Arabic and Persian. Arabic and Persian words became part of Pakistan's Islamic identity and provided the Arabic-based scripts of all Pakistani languages, thus forming a bond between different parts of the society.

From independence until the early 1980s, English was the language of choice in Pakistan's better schools because it helped students obtain admission to good universities in Britain, the United States, and Australia. Then, in a move to

# THE MYSTERIOUS KALASH PEOPLE

Located in the Hindu Kush mountain range near Pakistan's border with Afghanistan is an area called Kafiristan, meaning "Land of the Nonbelievers." The people of Kafiristan, known as the Kalash, have continuously rejected all efforts by outsiders to convert them to other religions; thus, Muslims call them "nonbelievers."

Today fewer than two thousand Kalash remain, distributed in three remote mountain valleys. Two of these valleys are accessible only by foot or perhaps by helicopter. The nearest city is Chitral, located in the North-West Frontier province.

The origin of the Kalash is a mystery, although many consider them to be descendants of the Greek armies of Alexander the Great (327 B.C.). This could be true because the Kalash are fair skinned and Alexander's army did pass through what is today northern Pakistan, but no absolute proof exists.

The Kalash live in beautiful, isolated valleys. Forests of holly, oak, and cedar grow at the base of the steep mountains, and the valleys are filled with fruit and nut trees. Clear, cold streams supply not only drinking and irrigation water but also power for small grist mills. Herding their goats and cows through this idyllic scene, the Kalash women, dressed in dark robes and seashell-decorated headdresses, add to the appearance of a fairy-tale setting.

In the 1990s, however, life began to change for the Kalash. Muslim groups have renewed efforts to convert them to Islam, and the Kalash have been treated harshly by overzealous, armed Muslim bands, who have seized Kalash property and built a mosque in one of their valleys. When the outside world learned of the plight of the Kalash, international human rights groups pressured the Pakistan government into creating the Kalash Foundation. Little has been done to help these people as of yet. Now there is a real danger that the unique culture of the Kalash, after surviving for thousands of years, may soon disappear.

*A Kalash woman and children take a break from gathering fruit during the fall harvest.*

promote national unity, the government of Mohammad Zia-ul-Haq declared that teachers in government schools must use Urdu. Zia-ul-Haq also mandated that Urdu be heavily promoted on television and radio. Urban private schools, where wealthy, educated parents send their children, were allowed to continue using English, and smaller rural schools still teach in the local languages.

At the start of the twenty-first century, the ethnic composition of Pakistan's 140 million people consisted of roughly the same proportions as the spoken languages: 58 percent Punjabi, 14 percent Pashtun, 13 percent Sindhi, 7 percent Muhajirs (Urdu-speaking Muslim immigrants from India), 5 percent Baluchi, and 3 percent are members of other ethnic groups. Each group is primarily concentrated in its home province, with most Muhajirs residing in urban Sindh.

Punjabis are not only the largest ethnic group in Pakistan, but they also dominate the upper levels of the country's military and civil service and essentially run the central government. Many Pashtuns, Baluchis, and (especially) Sindhis resent this unequal division of political power, and during the early 1980s mounting tensions led to violence between Punjabis and Sindhis. Despite all of the tribal diversity of Pakistani society, however, there is one common thread between all these groups: Islam.

## ISLAM IN PAKISTAN

Islam is one of the world's three largest religions and provides the foundation for much of what goes on in the daily life of Pakistan, where 97 percent of the population is Muslim.

Pakistan's Islamic society is based on the five pillars of Islam. These five mandatory duties of all Muslims include the believer's formal affirmation of faith in the teachings of Muhammad (the prophet of Islam), reciting prayers five times every day, fasting during the Islamic month of Ramadan, giving to charities, and making a pilgrimage to Mecca.

Like most religions, Islam imposes a code of ethical conduct that encourages generosity, fairness, honesty, and respect, and it guides believers on what constitutes proper family relations. Ethical conduct is codified in Islamic law, called *Shari'a*, which is as important as civil law in Pakistan. *Shari'a* specifically forbids adultery, gambling, charging high interest rates on loans, drinking alcohol, and eating pork and

blood; enforcement of *Shari'a* in Pakistan varies, though, often in response to the strictness of the current leaders.

*Muslim pilgrims, observing their religious duties, walk in the mosque at Mecca.*

## AN ISLAMIC SOCIETY

Pakistan was founded as a secular Islamic nation, meaning that religion was meant by the country's founders to be less a primary shaper of laws and government and more a reason for national unity and an ideal by which to live. During the early 1980s, however, dictator Zia-ul-Haq attempted with some success to change Pakistan into a more conservative Islamic state by reassigning government army positions to conservatives and developing thousands of religious schools (*madrassas*). Although Islam's *madrassas* have usually served a role of preparing religious scholars and clergy, many of the new *madrassas* formed during Zia-ul-Haq's era changed that time-honored function. They became the first step for young men on the road to becoming holy warriors, most of whom eventually went off to fight for conservative Islamic forces. Tens of thousands of Pakistan's former *madrassa* students joined the Taliban, a term meaning "student" (of a *madrassa*), who ruled Afghanistan for years, and many went to fight in Kashmir.

Zia-ul-Haq's legacy left Pakistan with a strong Islamic character. For example, women in the villages seldom are seen in public, and if they do go out, they are covered from head to foot in a veil called a chador. Even in the cities, where it is common to see women in Western clothes, most still dress conservatively. Mosques are full at prayer times, and even buses and taxis stop to let their occupants spread their prayer rugs on the ground and pray at the appointed times.

Quietly opposing the Islamic tide, however, are many Pakistani government and military people who believe the country's interests are best served by building enduring political, economic, technical, and military links with the United States and Europe. Indeed, President Pervez Musharraf reflected this when he explained why he had decided to side with the United States in its conflict with the Islamic Taliban regime in Afghanistan. Musharraf stressed that Pakistan's interests come first, even if it means opposing the Taliban, a tone that found increasing acceptance in much of Pakistani society during the beginning of the twenty-first century.

Highly conservative, militant Muslims are definitely an element of Pakistani society, but they represent only a small fraction of the country's population; from the 1980s to the

*Madrassas, like the one pictured here, provide a strict religious education to Pakistan's youth.*

present they have not attracted more than 5 percent of the popular vote. The leaders of the country's Islamic parties, however, are hoping that continuing government failure to adequately address severe shortcomings in public services will shift society toward their viewpoint. Nevertheless, Pakistanis will not allow anything to disrupt one element of their disparate society that is as much of a common factor as Islam: the family.

## FAMILY AND MARRIAGE

The family is paramount in Pakistani society, and social life revolves around family and relatives. For most Pakistanis, a web of family connections provides their identity and protection. They seldom live apart from their relatives, and even in huge cities both males and females usually live with relatives or friends of relatives. Children live with their parents until marriage, and married sons often continue to live in their parents' home with their wives.

Pakistanis are not viewed as full members of society until they are married and have children. The primary goal of marriage is to join two extended families, so the parents arrange most marriages. Since husbands and wives are seen as representatives of their respective families, romantic attraction is not normally considered a sufficient reason to marry in Pakistan.

In Pakistani society, only children from the father's side are considered relatives. Marriage with a cousin on the father's side is preferred, partly because property exchanged at marriage then stays within the father's side of the family.

The relationship between in-laws extends beyond the couple. Families related by marriage exchange gifts on important occasions, and if a marriage is successful, it will probably be followed by other marriages between the two families.

A woman's life is often difficult during the early years of marriage, as a young bride has very little status in her husband's household. She must obey her mother-in-law and often her sisters-in-law treat her poorly. If she married a cousin, however, her mother-in-law is also her aunt, and so her situation may be better. A wife gains status and power in her husband's family by bearing sons, which are prized because they will eventually marry and bring new wives into the family. Daughters, on the other hand, are considered

*Beautiful scarves and ornate jewelry are customary ceremonial attire for women in Pakistan.*

liabilities because they eventually have to be given away in a costly wedding. Consequently, Pakistani mothers usually prefer sons to daughters; after a son has married, it is common for the mother and son to remain close. Mothers, not wives, usually have the most influence over a man.

In Pakistan, Muslim marriages require a dowry, by which the husband's family pays a sum of money or goods to the bride. A rich dowry may include household goods, clothing, jewelry, and furniture, and these items remain the property of the bride.

## WEDDINGS

In Pakistan, a wedding is a major event. Preparations for a traditional Pakistani wedding, which includes a variety of ceremonies, colorful costumes, and expensive celebrations, usually take months. The wedding ceremonies take three days, with the preliminary and final events occupying the first and third days and the wedding itself taking place the second day.

The day before the wedding the wife and husband, in separate ceremonies, are each decorated with intricate henna designs on their hands. The bride wears a special yellow dress and no makeup for the application of henna. The event is accompanied by traditional songs and dances, and food is served.

On the wedding day, the bride's parents host a reception where the official paperwork is overseen by an imam (a Muslim clergyman). After the paperwork is complete, the bride makes her appearance wearing an embroidered dress and large amounts of jewelry. All of the female guests wear their finest clothes and jewelry, and the men, in a recent change from tradition, now usually wear Western-style suits and ties. The bride's family accompanies her to a stage where she takes

 ## *MEHNDI:* SKIN DESIGNS IN HENNA

In Pakistan, as well as in India and the Middle East, an ancient art form known as *mehndi* is still widely practiced. *Mehndi* is the most common name for the practice of decorating the skin with henna dye.

Henna dye, which is made from a type of plant, is applied as a paste to the skin. Designs range from large, thick patterns to delicate geometric designs to paisleys and lacelike drawings. Henna takes several hours to dry, after which the paste is scraped off to reveal the design. The completed *mehndi* resembles a tattoo with a color that can be anywhere from light orange to red to dark brown. Unlike permanent tattoos, the henna designs last less than three weeks.

In Pakistan henna may be used in many ways on either gender. Its most common application is on the hands and feet of women. The one Pakistani occasion that absolutely requires the use of *mehndi* is a wedding. During the multiday wedding ceremonies, henna is applied to the bride and bridegroom as well as to several members of the bridal party. To Pakistanis henna designs symbolize fertility and the enduring love between husband and wife. *Mehndi* offers an additional benefit in the hot climate of Pakistan: It cools the skin. A wedding tradition associated with henna requires that the groom's name be written somewhere within the intricate designs of the bride's *mehndi*. If he cannot find his name, it is said that the bride will have the control in the marriage.

her place beside her new husband, followed by a long photography session, which marks the end of the wedding day.

The next day the groom's side of the family holds a reception. Again, everyone dresses in fine clothes, often including gold threads in the fabric of the women's clothing. The bride also wears a special gold piece of jewelry that dangles between her pierced nostril and left ear lobe.

## WOMEN IN PAKISTAN

When Benazir Bhutto became Pakistan's prime minister in 1988, she became the first female leader of an Islamic state in modern times. Her role as prime minister and head of the prominent Pakistan People's Party gave the impression to many Westerners that gender differences in Pakistani society might not be as great as in other Islamic societies. Supporting that impression, politically prominent women are not new in Pakistan. Muslim women played a leading role in the struggle for independence and have been elected or appointed to positions in local, regional, and national governments throughout Pakistan's history. But nevertheless, these Pakistani female leaders are not typical, and usually their elections and appointments came out of ethnic and kin relations in which an appropriate male was not available for the position.

As Muslims, most Pakistani women continue to lead traditional lives. Islamic society discourages women from leaving the home and provides them with little chance of entering into professional fields of work. An average Pakistani woman will be married at the age of fourteen, give birth to nine children, be unable to read and write, and never work or study outside of the home.

Attempts by national and international development agencies to increase educational and healthcare opportunities for Pakistani women are impeded by Muslim attitudes toward women's roles in society. Even though Islam teaches that a woman has the right to run her own affairs, in practice few women act independently. This is because in Pakistan's Muslim society, most interactions between a woman and the outer world must take place through a male relative, and even then only after consulting with other male kinsmen.

The deeply rooted Muslim tradition that governs the lives of Pakistani women is known as purdah, which means "cur-

*A Pakistani woman decorates her hand with henna dye.*

tain or veil." Observing purdah essentially means keeping the genders separated, and unless they are close relatives, men and women must keep their distance from each other. Should a Pakistani female meet a male who is not a close relative, she must preserve Muslim modesty by avoiding eye contact, speaking formally, and keeping the interaction short.

In Pakistan's urban centers, many of the women from wealthy families no longer feel constrained by purdah. In cosmopolitan Karachi, Islamabad, and Lahore, women from the elite levels of society may be seen in the streets and stores unveiled, and sometimes they may even dress in Western styles. This would be most unlikely, however, in the provincial towns and villages. In Baluchistan and the North-West Frontier, to even see a woman out of the home is uncommon. When a woman does appear in public in these conservative areas, she is usually concealed by the all-enveloping burqa (like a pleated tent) or chador (a cloth wound around the head and body).

According to a 1999 report by Samya Burney of the international organization Human Rights Watch, "Women in Pakistan face spiraling rates of gender-based violence, a legal framework that is deeply biased against women, and a law enforcement system that retraumatizes female victims instead of facilitating justice."[5] With most women excluded from Pakistan's modernization efforts, many experts believe that the country may not see greater rights for women for some time.

### Education and Literacy

Pakistan's constitution guarantees free basic education for all citizens, although the country still has far to go in fulfilling this guarantee. Although Pakistan has many elementary and secondary schools and a handful of colleges and universities, there are not nearly enough for Pakistan's rapidly growing population, and most of the existing schools are in the cities and are only available to males.

*Girls study together in an open-air school.*

More than half of Pakistan's people are illiterate, and the situation is substantially worse for women than for men. In

rural Sindh, for example, only 13 percent of adult women can read, and in Baluchistan, the figure is 10 percent. According to the director of the country's literacy program, "There are about 55 million adults who are illiterate in this country. And as far as women are concerned, three out of four women in Pakistan cannot read and write."[6]

From its inception, Pakistan has given first priority in education to boys. Since Islamic societies do not allow coeducational schools, even for young children, and because many areas lack the resources to build more than one school, the number of schools for girls is far less than the number for boys. In addition, there is a persistent lack of qualified female teachers to staff the few schools that are available for girls. Furthermore, older girls are expected to help raise their siblings and do housework, which prevents attendance even when a school is available. Finally, many communities are apathetic about education and do not encourage children of either gender to attend, preferring instead to have the children help with caring for younger siblings, work in the fields, or enter Pakistan's extensive child-labor market.

A few nongovernmental organizations from other countries work in Pakistan to help raise the literacy rate. One such group is Development in Literacy, a cooperative venture between American and Pakistani women's organizations that operates schools for several thousand girls in rural Punjab and Sindh. Some of these girls attend in defiance of their father's wishes, and there have been incidents in which fathers have burned their daughter's books or beat their mothers for letting them attend.

Pakistan's government has become aware that more than half of the country's illiterates are adults, so it has begun to focus on adult education programs. Since most adults are busy trying to earn a living, however, getting illiterate adults interested and motivated enough to learn to read and write requires specially trained teachers and more money. Both are in short supply in Pakistan.

Pakistani society is rooted in the family. Pakistan's future, therefore, depends on preserving these roots by improving opportunities for all members of society—men, women, and children—while honoring the rich Islamic traditions upon which the country was founded.

# 5

# Pakistani Culture

Pakistan is an often bewildering array of cultural contradictions. A city dweller can eat at a McDonald's restaurant, watch MTV, make a call on a cell phone, read a *Vogue*-like Pakistani fashion magazine in English, drink a beer, and log on to the uncensored Internet. But less than half of Pakistanis are literate, alcohol is officially illegal, thousands of schools teach only the fundamentals of Islam, many tribal areas have no electricity, and city streets are lined with beggars. Perhaps the country's cultural essence is, as many Pakistanis themselves say, one of contradiction: West and East, traditional and modern, religious and secular.

### ARCHITECTURE

The blending of East and West in Pakistani culture is clear in the country's architecture. The Eastern influence is best seen in the many examples of architecture from the Mogul era, and these monuments, forts, mosques, and tombs remind modern Pakistanis that their country was once part of the most prosperous country on Earth. Mogul architecture was the dominant style of larger buildings when the British arrived and began to contribute their Western designs to Pakistan's architectural heritage. During the colonial period the British built elegant government buildings and monuments in Lahore and other major cities, most of which are still in use today.

Both the old Mogul styles and the more recent architectural developments incorporate elements of Islam, which continues to be the major Eastern influence on modern Pakistani architecture. Because Islam forbids artists and sculptors from depicting the human form, mosques and other Muslim structures do not contain pictures or sculptures of people. Instead, they are lavishly decorated with verses from the Koran (the Islamic holy book), geometric patterns, and flowers, often expressed with semiprecious stones and glazed tiles inlaid into the walls.

As modern Pakistan struggles to invent its own style of architecture, government and private businesses are erecting

*A Lahore mosque illustrates Pakistan's intricate style of traditional architecture.*

new buildings that blend elements of Western designs with the arches and domes of traditional Muslim styles. Many of the most notable examples are seen in the government buildings of the planned capital city, Islamabad, but even older cities like Karachi and Lahore are sprouting new commercial structures.

Even Pakistan's newest buildings usually incorporate elements of the region's traditional crafts, such as ancient design motifs and traditional woodwork. These structures pay homage to the country's arts and crafts as the strongest links to Pakistan's past.

## ARTS AND CRAFTS

The arts and crafts of modern Pakistan are heavily influenced by the Mogul period, even though it ended many hundreds of years ago. Art attained a remarkable level of refinement under the sponsorship of the royal courts of the Moguls. Mogul manuscripts were filled with Persian-inspired miniature paintings, a style that is widely copied today.

Modern Pakistani artists, less formal than their predecessors from the Mogul period, are gradually gaining an international reputation for expressing the spirit of a people struggling to find their place in the modern world; as of yet,

*Like many Pakistani crafts, traditional caps at a market in Islamabad are made using ages-old production techniques.*

however, there are no Pakistani painters of international stature. Several fine art schools and an established core of prolific artists are developing styles of painting that are uniquely Pakistani, exhibiting works that blend Western styles with Eastern topics and traditional motifs.

In modern Pakistan most jewelry making continues to reflect ancient styles. Jewelry making is one of the arts that reached a high level of refinement during the Mogul period, and today's gold chokers, bracelets, and earrings are often decorated with the same intricate engravings found on jewelry from five hundred years ago. This handmade jewelry is especially popular among many Pakistani tribal women, who commonly wear numerous bracelets and pierce the outer ridges of their ears so they can wear several hoops and ear studs at once. Rural Pakistanis, many of whom prefer to put their savings into jewelry rather than banks, are the main customers for bangles and necklaces featuring gold, pearls, and rubies. Even in the cities the demand for the traditional styles remains high, although Western-influenced jewelry designs and materials are increasingly being sought by sophisticated urban Pakistanis.

Using techniques that have hardly changed for a thousand years, Pakistani artisans create beautiful forms of pottery. Around the city of Hyderabad in Sindh, for example, river mud is formed into tiles, glazed in blue and white, and used to decorate mosques. Other Pakistanis use an age-old technique for making paper-thin pottery, and lattice designs used in these pieces make them seem almost like lace. Pakistan is also known for its black and maroon glazed pottery; lacquerware decorated in patterns of blue, mustard, and brick red; and pottery with inlaid pieces of mirror.

The Pakistani crafts industry produces baskets, carved woodwork, and engraved metalwork for both domestic consumption and export. Artisans create intricately woven baskets, mats, blinds, fans, slippers, and caps from the leaves of the date palms, wild rushes, reeds, and wheat stalks. Decorated basketry bearing intricate geometric patterns woven from dyed grass, reeds, and leaves is very popular throughout the country. The artisan's touch is also seen in traditional homes as well as some modern structures, where owners often prefer to use doors, window frames, and household articles incorporating the country's traditional style of highly carved and inlaid woodwork. Pakistanis are fond of using common household objects made of engraved metalwork that are almost identical to similar objects made hundreds of years ago, and gold and silver platters, trays, serving vessels, and chalices engraved with intertwined flowering vines are popular among wealthy buyers.

Pakistan's artisans are famous for their carpets and rugs. The Baluchistan and Sindh provinces are where most Pakistani carpets and rugs are made. Like most other rural crafts, these were produced originally for local use, but now they are exported in large numbers. Common designs include striped and banded backgrounds decorated with squares, stars, crosses, rectangles, and octagons inside intricate borders. Rows of stylized camels are popular among the Baluchi tribes. A regional specialty from Sindh is a soft leather rug embroidered with silk, gold, and silver. Floral carpets conceived in Persia and developed during the Mogul period are also popular, as are carpets bearing a vase-like central motif echoed in quarter circles in each corner. As the result of a thriving export industry, these Pakistani carpets are increasingly popular in the West. And while Pakistan is exporting carpets to the West, it is importing many elements of Western culture, including music, movies, clothing styles, and fast food.

## MUSIC

Until the early 1980s, the popular music of Pakistan consisted almost entirely of tunes from current Pakistani and Indian movies played and sung by local artists. It is only recently that large numbers of Pakistanis have started listening to Western-style pop music, a phenomenon spurred by the rise of Pakistani rock musicians.

In 1980 a thirteen-year-old Pakistani named Nazia Hassan revolutionized Pakistani musical tastes by blending Eastern and Western styles, and topping Pakistan's music charts in the process. This opened the door for Pak-rock bands, led by the most famous modern musical group in south Asia, Junoon.

Although Pakistani television provides uncensored news from outside the country, this does not mean that the government is entirely open-minded about the contents. When Junoon wanted to air its new music video on television, the

## NUSRAT FATEH ALI KHAN, PAKISTAN'S WORLD MUSIC STAR

No other Pakistani singer has enjoyed as much popular fame as Nusrat Fateh Ali Khan (1949–1997). His voice and his new arrangements of a traditional style of Islamic music acquired him millions of fans throughout the world.

Khan, born in Faisalabad, Pakistan, came from a family whose name is synonymous with the ten-centuries-old form of Islamic devotional music known as *qawwali*, a form previously associated with the Sufis. Until Khan popularized this musical style with his soaring voice, *qawwali* had seldom been heard outside of its traditional performances at Thursday evening sessions of Sufi congregations in Pakistan and northern India.

Through Khan's otherworldly voice, *qawwali* music was discovered by audiences far beyond the lands of its origins. British pop star Peter Gabriel brought Khan to the attention of Western audiences. As his fame grew, his music found an ever-widening audience. He sang with several rock musicians, sometimes offending musical purists back home in Pakistan, and his music was even featured on the soundtrack of the American movie *Dead Man Walking*. During his lifetime Khan was honored with numerous international musical and cultural awards.

Khan viewed himself as an ambassador carrying the most peaceful messages of Islam to the world and exposing his audiences to a positive image of Muslims. His music and amazing voice have been described as a bridge between all religions, spreading the message of peace and spirituality to everyone.

state-run television station turned the band down. Because the video made blatant references to the country's corruption and waste, a government official ominously advised the band to stick to entertaining and stop questioning the government. During the mid-1990s Junoon was banned from television and radio altogether, and authorities even tried to ban the group's concerts. It was not until Pervez Musharraf took over the government in 1999 that Junoon was able to perform in Pakistan again—the result of members of the general's family being big fans of the band.

*Qawwali* music (derived from the Arabic word for "belief") is the undulating devotional music of the sect of Muslim

## JUNOON

The most popular rock band in south Asia is a trio based in Karachi named Junoon. Junoon, whose name means "Passion" in the Urdu language, is more than a rock band; it bridges East and West, Islam and Christianity. Two members of the band are Muslims from Pakistan, and the third is an Irish Catholic from New York.

The three members of Junoon are long-haired rock and rollers who sound like Led Zeppelin, the Beatles, and U2 blended with Ravi Shankar and Nusrat Fateh Ali Khan. Although they sing mostly in Urdu, the two Pakistani band members speak perfect English peppered with the word *dude*, the result of growing up in New York during the 1970s where their fathers worked for Pakistan International Airlines.

Junoon emerged in 1990, during the most intense period of religious extremism in the history of modern Pakistan. The lyrics of many of Junoon's early songs attacked Pakistan's political corruption and protested nuclear proliferation.

After receiving recognition from the United Nations for their efforts toward peace in south Asia and on behalf of international AIDS organizations, in October 2001 Junoon became the first rock band to perform before the UN's General Assembly. The concert for peace was held in celebration of the fifty-sixth anniversary of the founding of the United Nations.

*Miles Shafin Ahmed is one of three musicians in the rock band Junoon.*

mystics known as Sufis. It originated during the tenth century as a blend of classical north Indian musical style and Persian and central Asian poetry and religion. *Qawwali* music, sung in Urdu, Punjabi, or Persian, is intended to elevate the spirit and bring both the listener and the singer closer to Allah (God). During the 1990s the popularity of *qawwali* music also grew, and today Pakistan's radio stations often alternate between rock and *qawwali*.

## TELEVISION

In a country with one of the world's lowest literacy rates, television is more than just a source of entertainment. It plays a crucial role in communicating news with speed and accuracy, replacing the traditional and less-reliable methods of gossip and one-sided speeches presented by traveling representatives of the various political parties.

Pakistan began black-and-white television transmission in 1967, and the first color broadcasts were in 1976. Today several commercial stations broadcast soap opera–style dramas, musical presentations, talk shows, news, educational programs, and sports events taped entirely in Pakistan, with the dramas being the most popular programming.

Most Pakistanis live in areas with television coverage, and like most of the world, watching television is a favorite pastime. Various transmission centers around the country provide the local announcers and dubbing necessary to broadcast programming in the nine major languages of Pakistan. Since 1992 Pakistan television has also broadcast via satellite to forty-seven countries around the world. These broadcasts have become very popular with millions of Pakistanis living abroad.

Not all of Pakistan television is on the government-owned PTV network. A private channel, Shalimar Television Network (STN), broadcasts a similar lineup of shows and movies in English from BBC, CNN, TNT, and other American and British sources.

## MOVIES

The United States has Hollywood, the Indian film industry has Bollywood (because it is based in Bombay, now called Mumbai), and the Pakistani film industry, based largely in Lahore, has Lollywood. Lollywood reached its peak during the late 1970s and early 1980s, when over a hundred Urdu and Punjabi films were released each year. During those years there were some nine hundred movie theaters throughout the country and eleven studios producing films. But the rising popularity of video has hurt the industry, and today the number of theaters has dropped to less than four hundred with only forty to fifty films made each year.

Pakistani movie theaters are huge air-conditioned buildings with special sections for families and provisions for eating

# THE POP ART OF LOLLYWOOD

Pakistan's film industry, known as "Lollywood," gave birth to what may well be the country's largest art form: the colorful hand-painted billboards that advertise new movies. With nearly fifty new Pakistani films released each year, Lollywood employs a large number of billboard artists.

Most of the movie billboards are painted in a complex of narrow streets in the old section of Lahore. There is hardly an inch of wall space to be found without some huge full-color hero glaring confidently at an imagined audience, gun or dagger in hand, in front of a mysterious or glamorous backdrop.

The artists design their billboards from pictures, posters, and film stills provided by the film producers, and a sketch of the artist's conception is approved by the producers before painting begins. The paintings are usually done on sheets of tin that are then pieced together to form one large billboard. The tin is first whitewashed before the picture is painted on it, panel by panel, using oil paints. The completed billboard will be mounted atop or in front of a movie theater. The largest billboards made by this method are almost five thousand square feet in size, almost as big as a football field.

Billboard artists often use garish color combinations to convey emotion and excitement. Sinister purples and greens are used to portray villains, and heroes might show up in blood-spattered white. Violence and heroism seem to dominate the posters, perhaps a case of art imitating life in this violence-prone land.

Unfortunately, this remarkable, home-grown art is slowly

disappearing as lithographs and computer graphics take over the billboard spaces. Printed billboards may portray the movie's characters more accurately, but they certainly lack the lively, kaleidoscopic feel of the creations of the street artists of Lollywood.

*A huge hand-painted movie poster covers a wall in Lahore.*

entire meals during the show. Pakistan's popular movies are almost always at least three hours long and provide an escape from both the heat and the drudgery of daily life. Most films are simple love stories with big dancing and singing scenes, lavish costumes, glamorous stars who sing popular ballads, bad villains, silly sidekicks, and never any on-screen kissing.

The Lollywood film industry exclusively targets Pakistani audiences; consequently, its movies have attracted little international interest. One Pakistani film that did become part of a major U.S. film festival was *Zar Gul*, which was featured at the DC Film Festival in Washington in 2001. Entirely different from the typical Lollywood commercial movie, *Zar Gul* was an action romance that dealt with politics, corruption, repression, and religious fundamentalism. Lacking significant exposure to Pakistani movies, Westerners know more about the country's sports.

## SPORTS IN PAKISTAN

Pakistanis are enthusiastic sports fans who are proud of the international success of some of their teams. The most famous sporting achievement for Pakistan was winning the Cricket World Cup in 1992, beating England, its former colonial master. But Pakistan is not a one-sport nation. In 1995 Pakistan had reigning world champions in four separate sports: cricket, field hockey, squash, and snooker (similar to pool). In fact, Pakistan has dominated the international squash circuit for almost two decades. In addition, Pakistan has won ten medals in Olympic competition, including three gold medals in field hockey.

Cricket originated in England during the sixteenth century and was brought to the subcontinent when India was a British colony. Two teams of eleven players compete against each other in this bat-and-ball game that is played during an October-to-March season. Whenever an important series is underway, fans throughout the country can be seen huddled around radios listening intently and roaring with delight at every run scored by their team. The excitement generated by a cricket game can go beyond the sport, as it did in 1986 when Pakistan for the first time defeated India in a series played on Indian territory. Given the history between the two countries, Pakistan's returning players were treated like war heroes. Polo, like field hockey played on horseback,

*Waqar Younis of Pakistan's cricket team delivers the ball to the opposing batsman in a game against Bangladesh.*

is another Pakistani sport with international implications.

Although polo actually started in Persia thousands of years ago, the sport was refined into its present form in Pakistan, eventually becoming one of the country's most famous exports. Afghans and Pakistanis love polo, and they play it aggressively, violently, and as close to horse-mounted warfare as one can get. The British picked it up while the subcontinent was a colony, and it quickly became the upper-class macho sport of Britain. In Pakistan today, polo is centered in the northwest areas of Chitral and Gilgit, where many of the players are soldiers and police officers.

Muslim clerics frown on the idea of women participating in any public sport that requires the athletes to play in relatively revealing clothing, a violation of Islam's teachings that a woman must always dress modestly in public. Consequently, few organized sports exist for girls or women. Sports will always be a major feature of Pakistani culture, but unless conditions change, women will participate only as spectators.

## CLOTHING WORN BY PAKISTANIS

From the tribal people in their traditional costumes to jeans-clad young urbanites, Pakistanis tend to be very clothes conscious. The majority of men and women still wear, at least from time to time, the national costume of a *kameez*—a loose long shirt with tails down to the knees— and baggy trousers called *shalwar*.

In the cities businessmen and government officials wear a shirt and tie in summer and a suit in winter. For several decades most men and many women in Pakistan's cities have been wearing Western-styles of clothes such as suits

# THE WILDLY DECORATED TRUCKS OF PAKISTAN

Trucks, called lorries in south Asia, are the most important means of transport in Pakistan, but they carry more than commerce. Pakistani truck owners cover their vehicles with painted images and decorations. As a result, truck art has asserted itself as the reigning king of Pakistani folk art.

Busy workshops around the country specialize in building, repairing, and decorating the cabs and bodies of Pakistan's huge fleet of trucks and buses. These shops supply the mechanics, welders, carpenters, painters, decorators, and materials to transform a ho-hum vehicle into a rolling art gallery. After the carpenters build the wooden bodies of the trucks, painters cover them with an amazing variety of images from the traditional to the ultramodern. When the painters finish, decorators add mirrors, ornaments, reflectors, chains, and an endless assortment of gadgets.

Truck artists do not seem constrained by the Islamic prohibition against portraying images of people. Pakistan's latest sports star, movie heroes like Rambo, and Muslim saints regularly show up on the sides of these trucks. Religious motifs are common, but no more so than pictures of women in both Western and Pakistani styles of dress. Landscapes and animals might appear on a panel right next to depictions of jets and automatic weapons. For a view into what is on the mind of a Pakistani lorry driver, one only has to look at his truck.

*This highly decorated truck, sporting the image of a jetliner, combines functionality with art.*

and dresses, but they still don the *kameez* and *shalwar* whenever they relax at home and for informal gatherings. More conservative Pakistanis, however, still prefer the *kameez* and *shalwar* because they fit the Koran's description of modest clothing, wherein women must keep their trunk, limbs, and at least the tops of their heads covered in public. Muslims are particularly opposed to women wearing short skirts, tank tops, and other clothing that shows a lot of skin. Even in less conservative Muslim families,

*Two Pakistani women in traditional garb offer a sharp contrast to the modern advertisement in the background.*

women are expected to wear lightweight scarves over their heads and shoulders when in public.

Although the *kameez* and *shalwar* are accepted everywhere in the country, each province and tribe has its own unique articles of clothing. For example, women from Sindh may be identified by their intricately embroidered dresses and colorful head scarves while Pashtun, Punjabi, and Baluchi men wear their own styles and colors of turbans. During various festivals and celebrations, city-dwelling Pakistanis who have stopped wearing their tribal styles in favor of jeans and T-shirts usually revert to traditional clothes. Like the mixture of traditional and Western clothing, Pakistanis have started eating Western food in addition to traditional cuisine.

## WHAT PAKISTANIS EAT

Pakistani food is similar to that of northern India, with a splash of Middle Eastern influence derived from other Muslim cultures over the centuries. Pakistani cuisine is based on curry or *masala* (hot and spicy) sauces that accompany chicken, lamb, and shrimp, along with a wide selection of vegetables, including lentil stew (*dhal*), spicy spinach, cabbage, peas, and rice. Pakistani meals almost always include baked and deep-fried breads (roti, chapati, puri, *halwa,* and nan). Many kitchens have a clay oven called a tandoor that is used to prepare delicious tandoori rotis and chicken.

The Pakistani versions of "fast food," the various lunches and snacks available from street vendors, include *samosas* (pastry filled with vegetables or meats and fried) and *tikkas* (spiced and barbecued beef, mutton, or chicken). Western and Chinese food is also widely available, and chains like McDonald's and KFC may be found in the cities. Islam forbids eating pork, so bacon and other forms of pork do not appear on the menus.

Proof that most Pakistanis have a sweet tooth is seen in their wide range of desserts. The most common sweet is named *barfi*, a confection made from dried milk solids. Other popular desserts are *shahi tukray* (slices of fried bread cooked in milk or cream, sweetened with syrup, and topped with nuts and saffron), *halwa* (made with eggs, honey, carrots, maize cream, and nuts), and *firni* (similar to vanilla custard).

*A type of bread called nan is a staple of the Pakistani diet.*

The most popular drink is tea (black or green), drunk strong with milk and usually very sweet. A drink made from yogurt called *lassi* is also popular. Western-style soft drinks are widely available, but alcohol, which is forbidden to Muslims, is only available to visitors with a special permit, and then only in upscale hotels and restaurants. Despite the ban on alcohol, beer is widely available, and only the most strict Muslims frown upon it.

All in all, Pakistanis are aware that they are incorporating significant elements of Western culture into their lives. Be it food, music, sports, or architecture, East is indeed meeting West in Pakistan.

# Domestic and International Challenges

Most Pakistanis want their country to be both a religious state and a secular one. And they want to be a modern nation bridging East and West, Islam and the world's other religions. To forge these divergent goals into a coherent, workable national policy is, as Pakistan has discovered, extremely difficult given the burden of the country's domestic and international challenges.

## The Ongoing Conflict in Kashmir

The state of Jammu and Kashmir is one of Pakistan's most pressing problems. When Kashmir was divided following partition in 1947, an agreement that was never recognized by Pakistan, the mostly Muslim state joined India. The United Nations has established a Line of Control separating the parts of Kashmir claimed by India, Pakistan, and China, a division that is still passionately contested by Pakistan. From partition right up to the present, Pakistan and India have maintained a military stance toward each other over the Kashmir issue, but China has avoided much interaction over the disputed territory.

The fact that Pakistan and India are willing to fight so long over Kashmir, a region with a small population and few natural resources, is difficult for many to understand. Kashmir's main asset is its beauty; it is located in a beautiful region of snowy mountains, green valleys, and abundant water between northern Pakistan and India. Kashmir attracted many tourists until the 1990s, when violence spread to formerly peaceful areas and drove them away. The region has little strategic significance for India, and Pakistan met its strategic needs in the Kashmir region soon after partition, when it conquered the third of Kashmir's territory closest to Pakistan's army headquarters in Rawalpindi. Rather than strategic concerns, it is religious ideology that is at the heart of the Kashmir conflict. Pakistan views itself as the subcontinent's homeland for Muslims, and so most Pakistanis feel Kashmir should be theirs. India, with its own large Muslim population, views itself as a land of diverse cultures; therefore, the fact that Muslims predominate in Kashmir is no reason for the disputed territory to belong to Pakistan.

Since both countries have steadfastly refused to back down from their claims on Kashmir, Pakistani and Indian troops have remained mired in a half-century-long military standoff at the Line of Control. Along this Line of Control, which happens to be on a high-altitude glacier, the two sides still frequently exchange fire with each other as they have done for more than fifty years. And inside Indian-controlled Kashmir, which makes up the largest part of the divided state, the periodic outbreaks of violence have killed thousands of people over the years.

*A Pakistani soldier in the disputed Kashmir region takes a break from fighting to offer afternoon prayers.*

Kashmir has already been the cause of two declared and several undeclared wars between Pakistan and India, and with both countries now nuclear powers, it is threatening to

cause another. In December 2001 Muslim terrorists attacked India's Parliament, an attack India blamed on groups fighting its rule in Kashmir and on Pakistan for supporting the attackers. India quickly massed troops along the border between the two countries, and Pakistan responded by bringing its own huge military force to the border. In an effort to diffuse tensions, President Pervez Musharraf quickly clamped down on Kashmiri militants operating within Pakistan's borders and outlawed Islamic guerrilla groups. Like all of the preceding actions carried out by other Pakistani and Indian leaders over the previous decades, however, Musharraf's actions had little effect on the continuing violence inside Kashmir or at the Line of Control.

At the end of 2001, faced with a frail economy that could ill afford more war and pressure from Western nations to stop supporting Muslim rebels operating in Indian-controlled Kashmir, Musharraf finally took significant steps to eliminate Pakistan's support of the rebels. He also called on outside powers to mediate a resolution of the dispute, but India rejected mediation because it would suggest that India's control over eastern Kashmir is negotiable.

The two countries remain locked in a stalemate, each with heavy military presence on their borders. India insists on maintaining the existing division of Jammu and Kashmir; meanwhile, Pakistan calls for United Nations–supervised mediation or elections to allow Kashmiris to decide who is to rule them, an idea opposed by India. The Kashmir situation has gone on for so long that many Pakistanis despair of it ever being resolved, as indicated by this 2002 statement published in a Pakistani English-language newspaper: "You have two countries that have positions that are irreconcilable. It's going to be one of those things that goes on forever and ever."[7]

Nevertheless, both governments have repeatedly declared that they want a peaceful resolution to the issues that divide them. Whether India and Pakistan can capitalize on that desire for peace, or whether the long hostilities will destroy any such initiative, remains to be seen.

## CONTROLLING THE MILITANTS AND *MADRASSAS*

Following the September 11, 2001, terrorist attacks on the United States, the role played by Pakistan in supplying

Muslim fighters to the Taliban, al-Qaeda, and Kashmiri rebel organizations became front-page news. Pakistan, the world learned, was home to thousands of *madrassas*. These schools had come under the control of extremists, who were using them to churn out thousands of militants for Muslim causes around the world, especially in Afghanistan and Kashmir. More alarming was the revelation that these extremists could conceivably seize power and turn Pakistan into a Taliban-like radical Islamic republic with nuclear bombs.

 ## HIGHLIGHTS FROM MUSHARRAF'S GROUNDBREAKING SPEECH

On January 12, 2002, Pakistan's president, Pervez Musharraf, gave a televised speech that was received with immense interest not only in Pakistan but in India and the West as well. (available in English at the Government of Pakistan website, www.pak.gov.pk). In it, he described a new direction for Pakistan that ended his nation's support for the Islamic extremists who were associated with terrorist acts.

I want to address the international community, especially the United States. As I have said before, Pakistan rejects terrorism in all its forms and manifestations. Pakistan will not allow its territory to be used for any terrorist activity anywhere in the world.

We have been taking measures against terrorism from the beginning, not because of any outside pressure. We were already carrying out these measures when a terrorist attack was carried out in America on 11 September. After 11 September we joined the international coalition against terrorism and I am delighted that the majority of Pakistani people supported this decision.

I however regret that some religious extremist groups resented this decision. I further regret that this opposition was not based on religious principles, but based on personal interests and party interests.

The majority of religious scholars are very enlightened people, but the extremists who are carrying out these protests think they are the sole custodians of Islam. They looked at the Taliban as if they were the renaissance of Islam and at those who were against the Taliban as if they

Musharraf responded to pressure from the United States and other Western countries to control the *madrassas* and prevent them from producing fighters for radical Islamic causes. Setting himself apart from other Muslim leaders and placing himself at great risk of being assassinated, Musharraf embarked on a clear and strong mission against Islamic extremism.

Musharraf gave a startling speech on January 12, 2002, in which he announced a reversal of many of Pakistan's recent policies. His words were cautiously welcomed by Western

were, God forbid, not Muslims. But these people have no respect for human rights . . . and the Pakistani people were let down by these so-called religious scholars.

First we have to rid ourselves of hatred, of religious intolerance. We have to rebuild and realize that a mind cannot be opened by oppression. . . . You cannot change hearts and minds through force. . . . We have the power to face external threats, but the danger eating us comes from within. . . . I appeal to my Pakistan to rise. To banish intolerance and hatred from ourselves and establish a climate of equality and brotherhood.

*Karachi shoppers pause to watch President Musharraf's speech outlining Pakistan's position on terrorism.*

countries. In the speech, televised live on Pakistan television, Musharraf focused on what he called the dangers of Islam's militant extremists, especially the dangers of such people controlling a large part of Pakistan's education system. Musharraf stated that although the *madrassas* normally serve an honorable role, in recent years most of those in Pakistan had been producing only semiliterate students of a narrow and extremist form of Islam, filled with hatred and ready to be sacrificed by non-Pakistani terrorist leaders. He ended his groundbreaking speech by reminding his country and the world that "Islam teaches tolerance, not hatred; universal brotherhood, not enmity; peace, and not violence."[8]

Musharraf immediately backed up his words with actions. Before September 11 he had lacked sufficient political support to oust the country's Islamic militants and Taliban supporters, who, he declared, were destabilizing Pakistan. With the majority of Pakistanis favoring the war on terrorism, however, he was finally able to fire the country's pro-Taliban generals and officials, put the leaders of militant Islamic political parties under house arrest, and shut down the most extreme *madrassas*. He also required all religious schools to register with the government, broaden their curricula beyond religious doctrine, and restrict their number of foreign students.

Musharraf achieved considerable success with his program to reform Pakistan's *madrassas* and his widespread efforts to curb the activities of Pakistan-based guerrillas. But Pakistan's tribal areas in the western mountains remain nearly lawless, and guerrilla and terrorist training camps there provide a much more difficult obstacle for any Pakistani leader committed to controlling the country's radical elements.

### HEALTH, POPULATION, AND POVERTY

Pakistan is a poor country with a population growth rate that is one of the highest in the world. The country suffers from substandard housing, inadequate sanitation and water supply, and widespread malnutrition, which all contribute to the spread of disease and to high infant, childhood, and maternal death rates.

Poverty impacts the health of a large proportion of Pakistanis. About one-third of the country's desperately poor millions live in the cities while the rest are rural residents. In the year 2000 about 13 million rural people had no access to health services, and only 45 percent of them had safe drinking water as compared to 80 percent of city dwellers, leaving 55 million Pakistanis without safe water. Only 10 percent of rural residents have access to modern sanitation compared to 55 percent of city residents, leaving almost 100 million people without adequate sanitation facilities. In addition, almost a third of the total population is unable to afford nutritionally adequate food.

Because of these conditions, the leading causes of death in Pakistan are gastroenteritis, respiratory infections, congenital abnormalities, tuberculosis, malaria, and typhoid fever. Malnutrition contributes substantially to the causes of death, and contagious childhood diseases are widespread, especially among rural children under the age of five.

Although the population has more than tripled between 1960 and 2000, and many health statistics have been discouraging, Pakistan has seen significant improvement in some health indicators. For example, in 1960 only 25 percent of the population had safe water, but by 2000 that figure had more than doubled. In addition, average life expectancy at birth was forty-three years in 1960, but by 2000 it had increased to fifty-nine years.

## The Growing Use of Tobacco

Smoking is another major health problem in Pakistan, where nearly half of all men smoke, and according to the World Health Organization, the number of female smokers is increasing. The national airline, Pakistan International Airlines (PIA), began a no-smoking policy on all of its domestic flights during the late 1980s, but in an unusual departure from global trends, PIA reversed this policy in 1992, claiming public pressure.

In addition to smoking, men commonly use *neswar*, a tobacco and lime mixture that is placed under the tongue. Many men and women also chew *pan*, a mild intoxicant consisting of betel nuts and herbs wrapped in a betel leaf. The dark red juice from *pan* damages teeth and gums, and stains from spitting *pan* are seen on sidewalks everywhere. Both *neswar* and *pan* are somewhat addictive and may contribute to oral cancers and other serious health problems.

### DRUG USE AND RELATED PROBLEMS

Opium smuggling and cultivation, as well as production of heroin from the opium, became major problems after the Soviet invasion of Afghanistan in 1979. The war interrupted the sources of opium in Afghanistan, and cultivators moved their operations to Pakistan. Although Pakistan's government cooperated with international agencies in their efforts to halt opium poppy cultivation, corrupt officials allowed the remote highlands of the North-West Frontier to become a major center of cultivation. Other parts of Pakistan increased heroin production in secret laboratories and served as a conduit for the drugs on their way to international markets.

*Heroin addicts loiter on a Karachi street.*

Not all of the heroin produced in Pakistan leaves the country. In 1980 heroin use among Pakistanis was almost unknown, but by 1991 there were more than 2 million users, with the increase most likely due to the increased availability of the highly addictive drug.

Increased heroin use introduced another problem in Pakistan: needle sharing, which in turn leads to diseases like hepatitis, tetanus, and acquired immune deficiency syndrome (AIDS). The effects of needle sharing among addicts, poor quality control of blood banks, and cultural and religious restrictions preventing the promotion of safe sex have combined to produce a growing AIDS problem. AIDS has not spread as fast in Pakistan as it has in other parts of the world, probably as a result of cultural mores limiting premarital, extramarital, and openly homosexual relations. But the World Health Organization estimates that in 1999 there were eighty thousand cases of AIDS in Pakistan, and the number is increasing.

## AN IMPROVING ECONOMIC OUTLOOK

Pakistanis earn an average annual income equivalent to about $400. This is very low by any standard, and the country's poor economic situation—given its combined external and domestic debt of $65 billion and the low income level—is likely to persist for many years to come. Nevertheless, Pakistan's industrial sector, which produces textiles, clothing, leather goods, carpets and rugs, sporting goods, machinery, and surgical instruments, is relatively strong and has the potential for high export earnings. According to analysts, Pakistan needs help to recover from several years of drought and past military expenditures. That help, in the form of loans from the International Monetary Fund and aid packages from the United States and other countries, had been held up by economic sanctions imposed after Pakistan's 1998 nuclear tests and subsequent unwillingness to sign a nuclear nonproliferation agreement.

The September 11, 2001, terrorist attacks on the United States also had economic implications for Pakistan. Many people in the West formed an image of Pakistan as an unstable breeding ground for Islamic extremists, an image that harmed the country's international business ties. Pakistani consul general Toheed Ahmad, whose job is to promote

*Workers stitch soccer balls in Punjab province.*

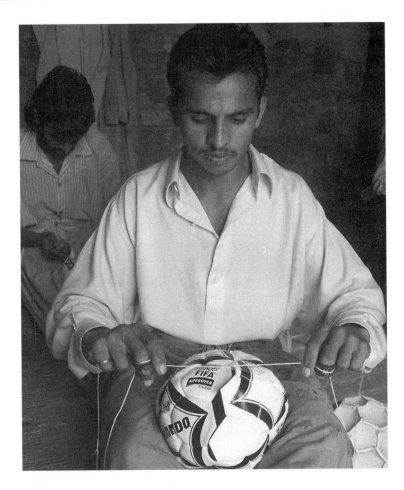

American investment in Pakistan's once-promising information technology industry, said a few months after the attacks, "Even if this war ends, it's going to take time to go to the USA and convince people we are civilized people, we are educated people, and we know the technology."[9]

Pakistan's foreign business fell more than 50 percent after the September 11 terrorist attacks. Hardest hit were the local divisions of international companies, especially in the clothing field, that have operations in Pakistan and the hundreds of Pakistani companies that depend on overseas sales. For example, Pakistan has about two hundred export-oriented software companies, and like other export industries in the country, new orders almost stopped after September 11. Pakistani business leaders are hoping that Musharraf's new policies in the wake of the attacks will help change the way

# VISIT PAKISTAN?

Pakistan is a land rich in natural beauty, cultural heritage, and intriguing historical sites. In a typical year, however, less than 10 percent of all foreign visitors to south Asia visit Pakistan, and about two-thirds of those go to Pakistan either on business or to see relatives. Why does such a beautiful country have so few tourists?

The answer becomes clear when one reads the travel warnings issued by the U.S. State Department. These warnings emphasize that crime is a serious concern for foreigners throughout Pakistan, with violent crime increasing faster than any other category. In the big cities—where poverty, high unemployment, and underpaid, undermanned police forces are the norm—carjackings, armed robberies, house invasions, and other violence against civilians are at an all-time high.

But tourists can also get into serious trouble outside the cities. For example, the U.S. embassy in Pakistan strongly discourages any travel to the North-West Frontier. Vast tribal areas in the province are outside the normal jurisdiction of government law enforcement authorities, and visitors risk being caught in armed clashes between tribal factions or smugglers.

With tribal warfare, robberies, and kidnappings commonplace, being a tourist in Pakistan has never been particularly safe. Now with a rise in drug and arms smuggling, anti-American sentiment, and members of the Taliban and al-Qaeda hiding out in the country, it is more dangerous than ever. A person intent on trekking in the Karakoram Range, shopping in the intriguing bazaars of old Lahore, or surfing on the perfect waves of Pakistan's coastline might be smart to wait for at least a few years.

*A young boy dries fabric outside of a sixteenth-century Lahore mosque. The scene illustrates the potential for beauty in this turbulent country.*

## AMERICAN SOLDIERS IN PAKISTAN

The United States has a long history of military cooperation with Pakistan, but the American-led coalition that toppled the Taliban regime and fought the al-Qaeda terrorist organization in Afghanistan also brought unprecedented numbers of American soldiers to Pakistan.

American and Pakistani military cooperation dates back more than four decades. During the 1960s Pakistan allowed American U-2 spy planes to take off from Peshawar for surveillance flights over the former Soviet Union. Then, when the Soviet Union invaded Afghanistan during the 1980s, American military personnel provided training, arms, and equipment to Islamic fundamentalist fighters based in Pakistan. As an American ally during the Gulf War with Iraq in the early 1990s, Pakistan sent a small military force to Saudi Arabia.

For half a century the United States has provided significant amounts of military assistance and funds to Pakistan. Then, during the late 1990s, with mounting evidence of Pakistan-based terrorist organizations and the development of a Pakistani nuclear arsenal, America imposed sanctions that effectively cut all military aid to Pakistan. Not until Pakistan offered its full cooperation following the terrorist attacks of September 11, 2001, did the American military return to Pakistan, this time in much greater numbers.

---

people perceive Pakistan and allow the country to return to its international business.

Musharraf's decision to back the United States and allow the American military to operate on Pakistani territory also had immediate economic results. The United States lifted the economic sanctions that had been imposed after the Pakistani nuclear bomb tests and promised substantial financial aid for Pakistan's ailing economy.

There may be a price to pay, however, if Pakistan becomes too friendly with the United States and other Western countries. Many Pakistanis already view the United States as anti-Muslim, partially because of American support for Israel and partially because of anti-American sentiments expressed by the country's Islamic militants. Consequently, any leader who encourages American intervention in what some consider Muslim affairs is sure to become unpopular with many Pakistanis. According to a BBC article written

Although exact figures are secret, news reports indicate that in the first months of 2002 more than thirty thousand U.S. military personnel were stationed in Pakistan, and American aircraft were using four bases in the Baluchistan province. Pakistan also granted permission to American troops on the Afghan side of the Afghanistan-Pakistan border to chase Taliban and al-Qaeda fighters into Pakistani territory. Furthermore, in March 2002 the United States asked Pakistan to lease it twenty-two thousand acres of land in Baluchistan to set up American military bases.

The continuing presence of the American military in Pakistan is a complex issue. People on both sides have expressed concern about the large U.S. military presence in Pakistan becoming permanent. India, another American ally and a frequent enemy of Pakistan, is not pleased with the prospect of U.S. military forces allied with Pakistani forces. Anti-American sentiment in Pakistan, which turned violent during the first months of 2002 (an American journalist was kidnapped and murdered and a church in Islamabad frequented by American diplomats was bombed), placed Americans at great risk. The issue of whether the U.S. military will remain on Pakistani soil may be one of the most controversial aspects of the war on terrorism.

shortly after the United States lifted its economic sanctions against Pakistan, "President Musharraf risks further internal strife if he is seen as being too close to the US, with many Pakistanis supporting the Taliban and Islamic fundamentalism. Such internal conflict could seriously damage the country's economy, potentially canceling out any benefits from the ending of sanctions."[10]

It seems clear that Pakistan is committed to becoming a modern, moderate Islamic nation. To stay on this path, Pakistan has established priorities of reducing the threat of war with India, controlling the violence of extremist and tribal elements within its own borders, improving literacy, reducing poverty, and stabilizing the economy. This young Islamic nation has already demonstrated that its people are resilient and determined, giving rise to the hope that Pakistan may soon rise above the daunting challenges it faces to take its place as one of the most important Islamic countries in the world.

# FACTS ABOUT PAKISTAN

## GEOGRAPHY

Border countries: Afghanistan, China, India, Iran

Total land area: 307,374 square miles

Coastline: About 500 miles on the Arabian Sea

Climate: Mostly hot, dry desert; temperate in northwest; arctic in north

Terrain: Flat Indus plain in east; mountains in north and northwest; Baluchistan plateau in west

Natural resources: Land, extensive natural gas reserves, limited petroleum, poor quality coal, iron ore, copper, salt, limestone

Land use: Arable land, 27%; permanent crops, 1%; permanent pastures, 6%; forests and woodland, 5%; other, 61% (1993 estimate)

Natural hazards: Frequent and occasionally severe earthquakes, especially in north and west; flooding along the Indus after heavy rains (July and August)

Environmental issues: Water pollution from raw sewage, industrial wastes, and agricultural runoff; limited natural freshwater resources; a majority of the population does not have access to potable water; deforestation; soil erosion; desertification

## PEOPLE

Population: 144,616,639 (July 2001 estimate)

0–14 years: 40.47% (male 30,131,400; female 28,391,891)

15–64 years: 55.42% (male 40,977,543; female 39,164,663)

65 years and over: 4.11% (male 2,918,872; female 3,032,270) (2001 estimate)

Growth rate: 2.11% (2001 estimate)

Birth rate: 31 births/1,000 population (2001 estimate)

Death rate: 9 deaths/1,000 population (2001 estimate)

Infant mortality: 80.5 deaths/1,000 live births (2001 estimate)

Life expectancy: 61.45 years

Ethnic groups: Punjabi, Sindhi, Pashtun, Baluchi, Muhajir (immigrants from India at the time of partition and their descendants)

Religion: Muslim, 97% (Sunni 77%, Shia 20%); Christian, Hindu, and other, 3%

Languages: Punjabi, 48%; Sindhi, 13%; Siraiki (a Punjabi variant), 10%; Pashto, 14%; Urdu (official), 7%; Baluchi, 5%; English (spoken by Pakistani elite and most government ministries), and other languages 3%

Literacy rate for those age 15 and over: total population, 64%; male, 51%; female, 77% (2000)

## GOVERNMENT

Form of government: A federal republic currently controlled by a self-appointed military president

Capital: Islamabad

Administrative divisions: 4 provinces, 1 territory, and 1 capital territory; Baluchistan, federally administered tribal areas, Islamabad Capital Territory, North-West Frontier, Punjab, Sindh (Note: The Pakistani-administered portion of the disputed Jammu and Kashmir region includes Azad Kashmir and the Northern Areas)

National holiday: Republic Day, March 23 (1956)

Constitution: April 10, 1973; suspended July 5, 1977; restored with amendments December 30, 1985; suspended October 15, 1999

Legal system: Based on English common law with provisions to accommodate Pakistan's status as an Islamic state

Suffrage: 21 years of age; universal; separate electorates and reserved parliamentary seats for non-Muslims

Executive branch: Following a military takeover on October 12, 1999, Chief of Army Staff and Chairman of the Joint Chiefs of Staff Committee Pervez Musharraf suspended Pakistan's constitution and assumed the additional title of chief executive; exercising the powers of the head of the government, he appointed an eight-member National Security Council to function as Pakistan's supreme governing body; President Mohammad Rafiq Tarar is the ceremonial chief of state

Legislative branch: Musharraf dissolved Parliament following the military takeover of October 12, 1999; bicameral Parliament, or Majlis-e-Shoora, consists of the Senate (87 seats; members indirectly elected by provincial assemblies to serve six-year terms; one-third of the members are up for election every two years) and the National Assembly (217 seats—10 represent non-Muslims; members are elected by popular vote to serve five-year terms)

Judicial branch: Supreme Court (justices are appointed by the president); Federal Islamic or Shari'a Court

Flag: Green with a vertical white band (symbolizing the role of religious minorities) on the hoist side; a large white crescent and star are centered on the green field; the crescent, star, and color green are traditional symbols of Islam

## ECONOMY

Gross domestic product (GDP): $282 billion (2000 estimate); real growth, 4.8% (2000 estimate), GDP per capita, $2,000 (2000 estimate)

Labor force: 40 million; extensive use of child labor

Industries: Textiles, food processing, beverages, construction materials, clothing, paper products, shrimp

Agricultural products: Cotton, wheat, rice, sugarcane, fruits, vegetables, milk, beef, mutton, eggs

Exports: $8.6 billion

Imports: $9.6 billion

Internet users: 1.2 million (2000 estimate)

# NOTES

### CHAPTER 2: FIVE THOUSAND YEARS OF CIVILIZATION

1. Allama Muhammad Iqbal, 1930 presidential address. http://users.erols.com.

2. Rahmat Ali, "Now or Never." www.slam33.freeserve.co.uk.

3. Quoted in Stanley Wolpert, *Jinnah of Pakistan.* New York: Oxford University Press, 1984, p. 133.

### CHAPTER 4: EVERYDAY LIFE IN PAKISTAN

4. Carol Lin, "Independent Spirit of Pakistani Tribe," CNN.com, November 7, 2001. www.cnn.com.

5. Quoted in Human Rights Watch, "Pakistani Women Face Their Own Crisis," October 19, 1999. www.hrw.org.

6. Quoted in Jeremy Bransten, "Pakistan: Government Launches Ambitious Program to Combat Illiteracy," Radio Free Europe/Radio Liberty. www.rferl.org.

### CHAPTER 6: DOMESTIC AND INTERNATIONAL CHALLENGES

7. *Pakistan Today,* "Searching for Answers in Kashmir," January 21, 2002. www.paktoday.com.

8. Pervez Musharraf, address to the nation, January 12, 2002. www.pak.gov.pk.

9. Quoted in *Saher,* vol. 5, issue 11, 2001. www.saher.com.

10. BBC News, "Sanctions Boost for Pakistan Economy," September 23, 2001. http://news.bbc.co.uk.

# CHRONOLOGY

**7000**

Bronze Age tribes live in Pakistan.

**ca. 3000–1800**

The Dravidian civilization inhabits the Indus valley.

**1800–518**

The Aryan civilization inhabits the Indus valley.

**518–327**

The Indus valley is ruled by Darius of Persia.

**327–325**

Alexander of Macedonia invades the Punjab.

**A.D.**

**1st–5th centuries**

Buddhist empire rules Punjab and nearby areas.

**Early 600s**

Turkish Muslims invade Punjab from Ghazni.

**644–711**

Muslim Arabs conquer Sindh and Punjab; large-scale conversions to Islam occur.

**700s–1300s**

Muslim rule brings stability and prosperity.

**1300s**

Mongol Huns invade and sack the Muslim empire.

**1400s**

The Mogul Empire is founded by Babur.

**1529–early 1700s**

The Mogul Empire thrives.

**1700s**

European traders compete for control.

**Early 1800s**

The British East India Company takes control of the former Mogul Empire.

**1818**

The Indian subcontinent becomes a British colony.

**Mid-1800s**

England subdues tribes in Baluchistan, Punjab, and Sindh.

**1893**

The Durand Line is formed.

**1906**

The All-India Muslim League is formed.

**1913**

Mohammed Ali Jinnah joins the Muslim League.

**1920s**

The Muslim League, under Jinnah, presses England for independence and separate Muslim and Hindu states.

**1933**

The name *Pakistan* first appears in a pamphlet written by a Pakistani student living in England.

**1940**

The Muslim League meeting in Lahore demands partition at independence.

**1940–1945**

Muslims from British India fight for England during World War II.

**1947**

Independence and the birth of Pakistan; Jinnah becomes governor-general of the new nation.

**1947–1948**

The first Pakistani-Indian war over Kashmir occurs.

**1948**

Jinnah dies.

**1955**

Iskander Mirza becomes governor-general.

**1956**

A constitution is adopted; Mirza becomes president.

**1958**

Mirza declares martial law; Mirza is sent into exile; General Ayub Khan assumes the presidency.

**1965**

A second war between India and Pakistan occurs over Kashmir.

**1969**

Martial law is declared; Ayub Khan resigns; General Yahya Khan assumes the presidency.

**1970**

The first general elections are held; Sheikh Mujibur Rahman's Awami League secures an absolute majority in the new National Assembly; the West Pakistan–dominated government declines to convene the assembly.

**1971**

East Pakistan attempts to secede; civil war begins; Bangladesh declares itself independent; India intervenes on behalf of Bengali separatists; Pakistani military surrenders to Indian armed forces; Yahya Khan resigns; Zulfikar Ali Bhutto becomes president of Pakistan.

**1972**

Bhutto and Indian prime minister Indira Gandhi sign the Simla agreement, which adjusts the cease-fire line between the two countries and creates the new Line of Control in Kashmir.

**1973**

A new constitution goes into effect; Bhutto becomes prime minister.

**1976**

Diplomatic relations are established between Pakistan and Bangladesh.

**1977**

General Mohammad Zia-ul-Haq removes Bhutto and proclaims martial law.

**1978**

Zia-ul-Haq becomes president.

**1979**

The Islamic penal code is introduced; Bhutto is hanged.

**1983**

Zia-ul-Haq announces that martial law will be lifted, says army will retain key role in future governments.

**1988**

Zia-ul-Haq and top military personnel are killed in a plane crash; elections are held; Benazir Bhutto is sworn in as the first female prime minister of a Muslim nation.

**1990**

National elections are held; Benazir Bhutto's party loses; Nawaz Sharif is elected prime minister.

**1993**

President Ishaq Khan dismisses Sharif's government, citing corruption; elections are held; Benazir Bhutto's party wins by a slim margin; Bhutto becomes prime minister again.

**1996**

President Farooq Leghari dismisses Benazir Bhutto, accusing her government of corruption and nepotism.

**1997**

National elections are held; Sharif comes to power again.

**May 1998**

Pakistan detonates three nuclear devices, bringing condemnation and sanctions from the United States and Japan and raising fears of a nuclear arms race in south Asia.

**October 1999**

General Pervez Musharraf topples the government of Prime Minister Sharif, accuses Sharif of massive corruption, destroying institutions, and undermining the constitution.

**June 20, 2001**

Musharraf appoints himself president; he later rules out elections.

**July 14–16, 2001**

India's prime minister Atal Bihari Vajpayee and Musharraf hold a series of talks on Kashmir.

**August 14, 2001**

Musharraf announces that national elections will be held on October 1, 2002.

**September 17, 2001**

Following terrorist attacks on the United States, Pakistan closes its border with Afghanistan to prevent more refugees and escaping Taliban fighters from entering Pakistan.

**September 19, 2001**

Musharraf pledges Pakistan's full support to U.S.-led coalition forces in their war on terrorism and allows American military into Pakistan.

**November 2001**

The United States lifts most of its sanctions against Pakistan and forgives debts worth billions of dollars.

### December 2001

Muslim Kashmir terrorists bomb India's parliament building; Pakistan is blamed.

### January 12, 2002

Musharraf denounces Muslim extremists and all forms of terror in a widely televised speech.

### Early 2002

Anti-American elements within Pakistan conduct terrorist actions against American targets, kidnapping and killing an American journalist and bombing a church in Islamabad.

# Suggestions for Further Reading

## Websites

**Dawn** (www.dawn.com). This is the online version of *Dawn*, an English-language newspaper that provides an excellent source of mostly uncensored news from the Pakistani point of view.

**Government of Pakistan Official Site** (www.pak.gov.pk). This is a fairly comprehensive site for all kinds of general information about Pakistan.

**The Hot Spot Online** (www.thehotspotonline.com). This is the site of an ice cream shop in Islamabad that is also a good source of cultural information about Pakistan.

**Pakistan Heritage Site** (www.heritage.gov.pk). This site offers a glimpse into Pakistan's history, culture, and traditions.

**Spider** (http://spider.tm/szone.shtml). This online version of the monthly magazine *Spider* carries cover stories and feature articles on the development of the Internet and how it affects Pakistanis throughout the world.

# WORKS CONSULTED

## BOOKS

Dennis Kux, *The United States and Pakistan, 1947–2000: Disenchanted Allies.* Washington, DC: Woodrow Wilson Center, 2001. This book provides a comprehensive and balanced survey of the ups and downs of U.S.-Pakistan relations during the first fifty-three years of Pakistan's existence.

David Low, ed., *The Political Inheritance of Pakistan.* London, St. Martin Press, 1991. This book presents some refreshing and insightful articles on the influential people and regions that contributed to the formation of modern Pakistan.

Ian Talbot, *Inventing the Nation: India and Pakistan.* New York: Oxford University Press, 2000. A good treatment of paths taken by these two sibling nations since independence.

Saeed Shafqat, *Civil-Military Relations in Pakistan: From Zulfikar Ali Bhutto to Benazir Bhutto.* Boulder, CO: Westview, 1997. This is an in-depth study of the corruption, abuses of power, cults of personality, and other aspects of the strange relationship between military and elected leaders that has haunted Pakistan since independence.

Stanley Wolpert, *Jinnah of Pakistan.* New York: Oxford University Press, 1984. This authoritative and insightful biography explores the public and private life of the leader who changed the map of the Asian subcontinent.

## INTERNET SOURCES

Rahmat Ali, "Now or Never." www.slam33.freeserve.co.uk.

BBC News, "Sanctions Boost for Pakistan Economy," September 23, 2001. http://news.bbc.co.uk.

Jeremy Bransten, "Pakistan: Government Launches Ambitious Program to Combat Illiteracy," Radio Free Europe/Radio Liberty. www.rferl.org.

Human Rights Watch, "Pakistani Women Face Their Own Crisis," October 19, 1999. www.hrw.org.

Allama Muhammad Iqbal, 1930 presidential address. http://users.erols.com.

Pervez Musharraf, English Rendering of Presidential General Pervez Musharraf's Address to the Nation. www.pak.gov.pk/public/President_address.htm

Carol Lin, "Independent Spirit of Pakistani Tribe," CNN.com, November 7, 2001. www.cnn.com.

*Pakistan Today*, "Searching for Answers in Kashmir," January 21, 2002. www.paktoday.com.

*Saher*, vol. 5, issue 11, 2001. www.saher.com.

U.S. Consulate of Pakistan, "Travel Warnings." http://travel.state.gov.

## WEBSITES

**Animal Information** (www.animalinfo.org.) This is a good source for information on rare and threatened animals around the world.

**Jammukashmir.net** (www.jammukashmir.net). This is an impartial site on the Kashmir conflict run by an expert on Kashmir at Kings College, London.

**Islamic Republic of Pakistan Official Website** (www.pak.gov.pk.) As the official website of the Pakistani government, this site contains a profile of President Musharraf as well as the text of his speeches.

**Pakistan Television** (www.ptv.com.pk.) A great source of current information and news, including video clips from Pakistani television.

# INDEX

# Picture Credits

# About the Author

William Goodwin writes about health, education, and other subjects for an online medical information service and a variety of other publishers. He is also a consultant and a speaker who has taught high school sciences, runs two businesses, built a large sailboat, and traveled throughout South America and Asia, including several trips to Pakistan. He earned a bachelor's degree from the University of California (UC) at Los Angeles and did his graduate work in biochemistry and later English at UC Santa Barbara and UC San Diego. He lives in the heart of Dixie in a house filled with females and love.